QUALITY IN EDUCATION

QUALITY IN EDUCATION THE QUALITY CIRCLE WAY

Deepa Sharma
and
Ravikala Kamath

Publications
KALPAZ PUBLICATIONS
Delhi - 110052

Quality in Education: The Quality Circle Way

ISBN : 81-7835-516-9

Rs. 450

Published in 2006 in India by
Kalpaz Publications
C-30, Satyawati Nagar,
Delhi - 110052
e-mail : kalpaz@hotmail.com

Laser Typesetting at : Vinayak Printers, Delhi
Printed at : Salasar Imaging System, Delhi

Contents

Foreword

Indian education is undergoing a silent transformation- concern for quantitative expansion steadily making room for quality of education. Ever since independence Indian education at all levels has experienced phenomenal expansion. Committees appointed by University Grants Commission expressed concern for quality in higher education from time to time. This was, however, not the case at other levels of education. Interestingly, quality of education did not find favour with the researchers for a long period. Though doctoral research in education began in 1943 in Bombay University, there is very little evidence of research on quality of education. It is only recently that the researchers have taken to research on quality in education.

There is lack of clarity as to what constitute quality in education. Literature on quality management is often evasive. To the extent, some authors claim that it is not particularly helpful to define quality; some resort to use of modified metaphor – quality lies in the eyes of the consumer (beauty lies in the eyes of the beholder). Most serious gap in quality in education is actual efforts and experimentations on quality management – whether quality can be changed in a planned experimental format.

Dr. Deepa Sharma and Prof. Ravikala Kamath's book fills that important void; it is based on their empirical research. The special feature of their research is experimenting with 'Quality Circle' approach for enhancement of quality in selected educational institutions. This is a significant departure from other contemporary Indian research on quality in education that are usually restricted to surveys. The authors have successfully demonstrated the effectiveness of quality circle approach as an effective tool for quality improvement through participative processes. In the process, they have developed some useful tools for measuring the developments in quality in educational institutions.

Dr. Sharma and Prof. Ravikala Kamath's book is educative. It is an important contribution to the growing literature in quality management in education. I congratulate and thank Dr. Deepa Sharma and Dr. Ravikala Kamath for making this important contribution to the issue of quality in education.

NIEPA, New Delhi

Marmar Mukhopadhyay

Preface

'Once upon a time there was a calf. One evening she walked home through a thick jungle. The distance to her home was only one mile but she walked three since, like all young ones, she wandered here and there, left and right, up and down.

The next morning a shepherd's dog passed that way and saw the calf's hoof marks and followed the path of the calf through the woods. Shortly after, the first sheep of a flock followed the path and behind him all the sheep. Thus a path through the woods was made.

Men began to use that path, cursing its twists and turns as they did but doing nothing about it. The path gradually became a lane, the lane became a road and horses and bullock carts followed it – followed the steps of the wandering calf.

A long time later the road became a street, and then a city's crowded thoroughfare, with thousands following in the footsteps of the wobbly calf.

Several decades later the road became the main street of a very large city. Buses, lorries, trams and cars followed the path of the zigzag calf, cursing the authorities and wasting precious time and money. But they all followed the same path'.

Often, in education, we are tempted to take the beaten track. Introduction of quality methods to education will open new vistas, engender new thinking, facilitate new roles and foster new functions. Let us make a new, challenging path!

Deepa Sharma
and Ravikala Kamath

A Word

Education that reaches beyond the ambit of mundane classroom teaching and brings about transformation is the key to all future development. This new vision of education enables the student population to benefit in the new environment, enables the teaching fraternity to function creatively and competently and presupposes the adoption of new initiatives and practices of human resources that can transform the system. It emphasises a holistic, interdisciplinary approach to developing the knowledge and skills needed for future as well as changes in values and behaviour. In this context and at the present juncture, Quality Circles (QCs) can and should play an integral part in the quality enhancement initiatives in education.

The National Assessment and Accreditation Council (NAAC) in India has stressed both maintenance and accelerating quality education and has been playing a catalytic role in achieving the goal of excellence. NAAC advocates among other modalities, initiating and sustaining 'Quality Circles' for quality enhancement in educational institutions. In the endeavour to promote effective mechanisms to start and maintain QCs, the need for basic, brief and precise 'know-how' for the same assumes vital relevance. This volume is an attempt to reach out to all stakeholders in education by providing the 'guidelines for QCs'.

This book has emerged as a result of eight years of research during which the authors were deeply involved in initiating, nurturing, monitoring and spreading QCs in different institutes of higher education and secondary schools. The book is primarily aimed at the stakeholders of education namely educationists, administrators, teachers and students. The central theme of the book is quality enhancement in education through QCs. The salient objective is to introduce, stress the concept of QCs and provide the know-how for initiation of QCs in education.

The book is divided in two sections. The first section deals with the theoretical, and philosophical aspects of quality circles. The second section gives concise information on 'how to' initiate Quality circles and address problems that might arise. The authors have deliberately chosen to present the matter in a simple but yet comprehensive manner.

Let us indeed march forward together on a new path leading to greater excellence in the field of education.

Deepa Sharma
and Ravikala Kamath

A Special 'n' Heartfelt Thank You to...

We wish to express our deep gratitude to the Almighty for the patronage and support through all the challenges faced during our research work and the compilation of this book. In addition, the warm blessings and encouragement from our seniors, elders and colleagues were the source of our strength and conviction to carry on even in adverse times.

The writing has been a humble reminder that our accomplishments are not ours alone. We are deeply indebted to more people than we can name. The Principals, staff and students of the educational institutions where data collection was done; dynamic friends from Mukand Steel Ltd. viz Dr. R.H.G. Rau, Mr. K.G. Kothari and Mr. M. Karkera particularly merit a huge Thank You for "being there" at all times of our need.

Special thanks are due to Dr. Maurice Holt (Professor of Curriculum Theory, University of Colorado), Dr. Robert Manley (Superintendent, West Babylon School District, New York) and Dr. Donald Dewar (President QCI International, Cotton Wood). Simple request note from absolute strangers elicited special suggestions and deeper insights despite their exceedingly engaging work programme. We thank them for their generosity and magnanimity.

Thanks are also due to Dr. Marmar Mukhopadhyay, Director, National Institute for Educational Planning and Administration (NIEPA) – India, for his encouragement and for writing the foreword at such short notice.

We would like to acknowledge the contributions of Dr. M.I. Patel, who by virtue of just-being-the-way-he-is has provided inspiration to the work. His eye for detail and zest for infusing quality in every task he undertakes taught us the deeper meaning of quality.

Our families deserve a special mention for being great morale boosters. They merit a special honour for putting up with our fluctuating moods and taking up the thankless tasks of photocopying, typing, and at all times being patient supporters.

Deepa Sharma
and Ravikala Kamath

SECTION – I

1
Quality and Education

"Would you tell me, please, which way I ought to go from here?" (Asked Alice)
"That depends a good deal where you want to go to", said the cat
"I don't care where.........." said Alice.
"Then it doesn't matter which way you go", said the cat.
(Lewis Carroll, in 'Alice In Wonderland', Chapter 6)

Does the education sector too suffer from a similar kind of aimlessness? If an industry made products that had little demand, had few takers and the users were required to mould and modify the product before putting to use, that unit would shut down in no time. Yet, institutions of learning do so without facing a similar predicament. Education produces students with certificates but not necessarily employability, students with grades but no creativity, students with degrees but not knowledge. Industry very often has to spend precious time, money and energy in "undoing, modifying and redoing" what is learnt at educational institutions.

Education needs to be more dynamic, self-corrective and self-invigorating process where every student gets the right kind of experiences to perceive one's own role as a contributor to the expansion of ideas, goodwill and harmony in a world replete with conflicts and contradictions. Education must contribute on the one hand to cultivating the mind and on the other to social change and development.

If education has to play a role beyond mere information relocation and certification, a rejuvenation of the system with a drive towards quality is the need of the hour. Conscientious and conjunctive efforts addressed at the immense education system are vital, not only to encourage optimal performance but also to ensure better products capable of independent, analytical thinking and enthused for constructive creativity based achievement.

The Mystique of Quality

The term "Quality" lends itself more easily to description than to definitions as aptly indicated by Pirsig (1976)....

"Quality.... you know what it is; yet you do not know what it is. But that is self-contradictory. But some things are better than others, that is, they have more quality. But when you try to say what quality is, it all goes poof! There is nothing to talk about. But if you cannot say what quality is, how do we know that it even exists? But we know that it exists. Why else would people pay fortunes for some things and throw others on the trash pile? Obviously some things are better than others... but what is betterness? So round and round you go, spinning mental wheels and nowhere finding any place to get traction. What on earth is quality?"

This is the "you-can-not-define-it-but-you-know-it-when-you-see-it" argument. Most debates on quality end up with the conclusion that Quality and Excellence are synonymous. There is also the notion of quality as confirmation to a standard or specification (NAAC, 1995).

Yet many definitions of quality prevail with varying degrees of tacit appropriateness. Some of them are:

Quality is...

- ➢ The fitness to use and conformance to requirement (Juran, 1984)
- ➢ A predictable degree of uniformity and dependability at low cost and suited to the market (Deming, 1986)
- ➢ The totality of features and characteristics of a product or service that bear on its ability to satisfy stated or implied needs (American Society for Quality Control, 1990)
- ➢ A perception arising as a consequence of how well a company meets all explicit and implicit promises made to a stakeholder. (Feigenbaum, 1995)
- ➢ A function of competencies in terms of knowledge, skills and attitudes, capacity and competition vis-à-vis needs (Goel and Biswal, 1996)

- A product or service possesses quality if it helps somebody and enjoys a good and sustainable market (Deming, 1997)
- Resultant from the system that produced it, and is an attribute of that system as much as of the product itself— of its processes, its people and the way they work together. (Holt, 1998)
- Efficiency in meeting the set goals, relevance to human and environmental needs and conditions and "something more" in relation to the pursuit of excellence and human betterment. (Rajput and Walia, 1997)

Quality becomes a problem when thought of as requiring a separate effort from managing the enterprise; when it is made very 'technical' with statistical tools and analytical reasoning. Quality is not an added feature to a product but a component of the product itself (Crosby, 1984). Quality is an achievable, measurable, profitable unit that can be achieved when one has the commitment and understanding and is prepared for the hard work. Quality enhancement cannot be achieved as an administrative process- it is a participative process involving various units of the institution (Stella and Gyanam, 2004).

Myths about Quality

There is a growing enthusiasm (and concern) for embracing the 'quality culture'. People venture to attain as close as possible to 100 per cent quality, not even 99 per cent. Because 99 per cent is not good

Table 1: Myths about Quality

- *Quality originates in quality departments.*
- *Training for quality is an expense and the upfront costs of quality are high.*
- *An expectation for perfection is unreasonable (Nobody is perfect).*
- *Quality improvements are made in small, incremental stages of 1 or 2 per cent and they never last long.*
- *Quality takes extra time and anyway it is innate.*
- *Quality programmes are fit only for industries (manufacturing processes).*
- *Quality is intangible so hard to measure but money is easy to measure.*
- *Workers are the root cause of quality related problems and they work their best when there is fear.*
- *Quality means goodness and is a luxury.*

(Galvin, 1995; Feigenbaum, 1995; Dror, 1995 Crosby, 1996).

enough! For example, 99 per cent level of quality, mathematically, would mean some 20,000 cases of wrongly dispensed prescriptions every year, 15,000 babies being accidentally dropped at birth by doctors or nurses, two long or short landings at major airports everyday, 500 incorrect surgical operations every week and 2000 lost articles in mail per hour! (Bagchi, 1996)

Improving quality is probably the most vital task facing any educational institution and hence quality must assume top priority in most agendas and action plans. The elemental aim of the quality movement in education is to help students and academicians alter the way they think about their work, the way they execute it and how they treat one another. Every piece of office work not done to the utmost potential of the staff's ability must be looked upon as compromising to the integrity of the staff. Every lesson not prepared and not taught to the best of the teacher's ability compromises the integrity of the faculty member and educational institute.

Thus Quality in education implies a philosophy that aligns the activities of all the key people in the education system with the common focus of customer satisfaction through continuous improvement of the educational system.

Education - Under Scrutiny for Quality

Earlier the issue of quality in education was regarded as nation-specific and culture-sensitive. Curricula were thought to be the concern of individual nations and local governments were obsessed with protecting "their" education from foreign scrutiny. Today the reform and intervention experiments have led towards a view that, although cultural differences remain, the quality of education can and indeed be subjected to technical scrutiny for educational objectives, purposes and improvements.

In recent years the meaning of academics has undergone a sea change. It is no longer just a way for 'getting a degree' or 'just going to school'. Education is a big sector that is frequently the nation's largest employer, it typically accounts for "an average of 27 per cent of national income, 15 per cent of a nation's resources, 25-30 per cent of public sector employees and on any given day, it directly involves a substantial portion of a nation's population" (Shelton, 1995).

In the modern world of diminishing resources, as a matter of policy, every organization has necessarily to be "quality conscious". Today, with rising costs, emphasis on value for money and focus on issues like transparency in the system, accountability and cost effectiveness, there is imperative need to pause, introspect and scrutinize education for quality.

Quality Initiatives in Education

Quality in education is of comparatively recent concern. Wisconsin, which is the sixth largest university in the U.S., and one of the largest public research universities that has turned out some of the most visionary leaders in business, science, education including Nobel Prize and Pulitzer Prize winners undertook quality initiatives. At that time one question asked was, 'If U.S.A. has the best education in the world and if Wisconsin is world class, then why should we change what we are doing now?' The answer given was "That's exactly what they said about the American Auto industry thirty years ago" (Shalala, 1995).

As the term "quality" is associated with industry, it reminds one of business units and production systems, giving rise to the debate regarding the role of quality in education. Is education business? Does it need to be "managed"? Should a "noble" profession like education be treated like business?

The crux of the issue lies in the interpretation of the term 'business'. If by the term "business" one implies inhumane and cold environment with focus on profits, expense control, budgeting systems than it is to be dreaded. If on the other hand, business implies greater teamwork, greater coordination, empowerment of the suppliers and recipients of education and relevant education then it has to be embraced wholeheartedly. And modern day business is concerned with "employee-empowerment, enhancement of work environment with various schemes for worker-enrichment".

So, education does need to be managed like business, at least the economics of education needs to be addressed. Almost all the quality management techniques have emerged in the industrial sector that have subsequently been extensively experimented and used in education and service organisations (Mukhopadhyay, 2000). Education can benefit from quality enhancement techniques practiced in industry because of the increased emphasis on quality and customer satisfaction.

Quality management is a process of change with the following basic characteristics:

- Starting from the customers' or users' point of view-whether staff, student or member of the public
- Redefining the role of the organizational culture and the administration
- Building commitment to quality in the work force
- A change in values and responsiveness by top management
- Empowerment of the staff to analyze and solve problems
- Emphasis for problem characterization on the system rather than the individual
- Emphasis on collective responsibilities, planning, benchmarking and managerial leadership
- Modifying the reward system
- To enable every intended functions to achieve expected results.

(Billing, 1996; Indiresen, 1996; Jayakody, 1996; Rajput & Walia, 1997 and Patrick 1999).

In education, various inroads to quality concepts and initiatives have been made, for e.g. TQM (Total Quality Management) in Education, TQE (Total Quality Education), CQI (Continuous Quality Improvement), Quality Circles etc. Though the modus operandi of these inroads may differ, the basic underlying principles are the same. They are:-

(1) ***Long term planning.*** The organisation needs to plan for today keeping the future in sight. An establishment needs to maintain its competitiveness, in its organisational environment by determining where the organisation is, where does it want to go, and how to get there.

(2) ***Customer Focus.*** The customer is the king. The entire process of quality management focuses on one issue-the needs of the customer, both internal and external.

(3) ***Continuous Process Improvement.*** Quality is not an end product; it needs constant and continuous working upon. This can be achieved through Kaizen, QC, (Dale, 1999) etc. There has to be continuous performance appraisal and skill building.

(4) ***Management by fact.*** The modern management functions with a scientific approach rather than the ancient dogmatic, fixed and feudal way. It is imperative to handle

issues and concerns with data and logical reasoning.

(5) ***Empowerment.*** Participatory management results in empowerment. The delegation of power at frontline levels (say, teachers for example) results in responsibility of outcomes and a sense of ownership.

(6) ***Human Resource Development.*** The need for new knowledge, new skills exist not only for the students but also for the teachers. To provide for a conducive environment for the development of human resource potential is the responsibility of the management.

(7) ***Teamwork.*** Working in teams result in better relationship between the employees leading to better work environment. Care should be taken to also have cross-functional teamwork.

(8) ***Managerial Leadership.*** In a quality focused organisation, the management and leaders work in unison. Management is necessary for coordinating people and resources and creating order and stability while leadership copes with change. Without management, change may not be relevant to the organization's vision and goals. Without leadership, the organization remains stagnant and creative solutions may never be implemented.

Educational practices can hardly afford to be static in the midst of fast changing world. Education is not exempt from the rising expectations of quality. In fact education should be at the vanguard-learning, researching and adapting, adopting and teaching new knowledge. Education sector is awakening towards quality consciousness and quality initiatives. Quality initiatives, if implemented in the right way, with the right perspective and with appropriate training are bound to be a resounding success.

Although, many options for founding quality are available, the choice of suitable quality strategy and appropriate implementation is of utmost important. Haste may be ineffective, costly and frustrating. The rhetoric of crisis may lead to half-baked solutions.

2

Quality- Perspectives in Practice

Education is what remains with you,
After you have forgotten everything you learnt.

Schools and educational institutions need to spell out and address educational goals. They may broadly encompass one or many of the following dimensions:

- Comprehensive education (a generic, enlightened orientation that enables expansion and intelligent, realistic application).

- Basic knowledge and its components (fundamental competence and skills in the areas of the languages, the arts, history, science and technology, mathematics and practical living).

- Specialised skills necessary for utilisation of some prevailing technologies (for instance; command in using electronic systems).

- Social competence (social-ethical judgment and action, social cooperation).

- Ability to manage life (emotional, cognitive and social adeptness to handle the challenges of life).
- Better quality of life and that guarantees an enlightened human being.

To achieve these educational aims, the mode of traditional learning must be supplemented and partially replaced by advanced methodologies; the traditional patterns of instruction must give way to newer pedagogical alternatives. Even way back in 1972, the International Commission on the Development of Education declared "democracy's keystone is education; not only education that is accessible to all, but education whose aims and methods have been thought out afresh." Education assumes an even greater role in countries (like India) where it contributes to reduction of poverty by increasing the productivity of labour, by reducing fertility and improving health, and by equipping people to participate fully in the economy and in society (World Bank Review, 1995).

Concern for quality in education is of recent origin, especially in India. So far, it was accepted that the quality of educational programmes are to be judged and decided by the academic community in the university and the autonomy of the university does not allow outsiders to interfere in any way in this function (Takwale, 1996).

The scenario is changing substantially during recent times. For the first time in the history of Indian education, universities are called upon to 'earn' their money. One third of the grants they get now from the government will be linked with performance and judged by University Grants Commission (UGC).

Government recognition to the primary and secondary schools is decided on the basis of report given by the inspection committee about the schools. The financial assistance to 'government aided' schools also depends on the grades awarded to the school (Government of Maharashtra, 1979). Several bodies at national and state level have been created to ensure the standard of quality and knowledge imparted to the students at secondary school level. The foremost among such agencies is NCERT (National Council of Educational Research and Training) and SCERTs (State Council of Educational Research and Training). The COBSE (Council Of Boards of Secondary Education) plays a coordinating role of standards of curriculum prescribed by the different boards of Secondary Education and implemented by Secondary schools in the respective states (COBSE, 1995).

For maintaining quality and standards in Higher Education, various councils have been established like AICTE (All India Council for Technical Education), MCI (Medical Council of India), NCTE (National Council for Teacher Education), DEC (Distance Education Council) and NAAC (National Assessment and Accreditation Council).

National Board of Accreditation (NBA) for AICTE came into existence in 1993 and deals with technical, management and pharmaceutical education. The procedure of accreditation envisages furnishing of data by the institution on various preset criterion, recommendatory decision about the accreditation by the sectorial committee to the board and the final decision by the board. Accreditation is accorded for a period of 6 years with grading 'A/ B/C' and 'no accreditation' based on cumulative index. There is also provision for a short duration accreditation and for a review of accreditation action taken by the Board.

National Assessment and Accreditation Council (NAAC), an autonomous organization, established by the U.G.C. on 16th Sept. '94 has its headquarters at Bangalore. It deals with natural sciences, humanities and social sciences, arts, law, commerce and other areas in liberal arts. Its prime agenda is to assess and accredit institutions of higher education. The institutions undertake self-study on the basis of set parameters and submit the report to the peer review team. The institutions are assessed with the basic aims of ensuring continuous improvement in the entire operations of the institution and to assure everyone connected about the accountability of the institution for its own quality and probity.

Education system does not function in vacuum but is a part of the larger social system. Policy changes like liberalization and privatization have their impact on education system. And then, with the globalization of the economy, can education be far behind?. 'The transition to 'one world' is a painful process, for the vital question is who gets integrated into whom. Obviously, the weaker gets subsumed into the stronger....', (Mukhopadhyay, 1997) Hence, there is a crucial need for introspection. With the foreign universities opening more and more centers in India coupled with aggressive marketing strategies, Indian education can only retain its identity and integrity if it can provide a world-class quality of education.

Quality Assurance and Control Systems in Education

For offering quality in education, each school must optimize on its own potential (Mukhopadhyay, 2001). Various concepts like TQE, TQM, CQI have been widely explored in education. Increasingly education institutions are also applying for certification of standards as in industries - for, e.g., BS5750. ISO 9000 series is also finding its way to many educational institutions. The Malcolm Balridge National Quality Award, an annual award recognizing U.S. companies that excel in quality management and achievement was expanded to include a category for education in 1993 (Arcaro, 1997 and Horine, 1999). Some Indian educational institutions like BITS (Birla Institute of Technology and Sciences) Pilani have got ISO certification.

The continuing concern for quality of higher education in India has projected the need for evaluation of performance of universities and colleges. This has led to the establishment of NAAC, with the prime agenda of assessment and accreditation of institutions of higher learning.

NAAC is a member of International Network for Quality Assurance Agencies in Higher Education (INQAAHE) and accredited status has been given to many Universities and colleges from all over India. NAAC has developed a five-step process for assessment and accreditation (NAAC, 2000).

(A) The institution/programme volunteering to be accredited would undertake self study to survey the existing situation, analyse the areas of strengths and weaknesses along with the plans to deal with the weaknesses, improvement, updating of existing programmes, diversification into new programmes and modification of irrelevant or obsolete ones. The parameters for assessment broadly include:

1. Curricular Aspects
2. Teaching, Learning and Evaluation
3. Research, Consultancy and Extension
4. Infrastructure and Learning Resources
5. Student Support and Progression
6. Organisation and Management
7. Healthy Practices

(B) The completed self-study would be analysed internally by the NAAC.

(C) The peer review team would visit the institution.

(D) The report of the team along with the self-study

report would be further studied by the NAAC.

(E) The Executive Committee of the NAAC would review the report and communicate the decision on accreditation to the institution.

Quality Management in Education

Educational institutions can gain a lot from industries. Diwan (1995) and Choudhary, (1996) have compared the characteristic features of a quality institution with that of an ordinary institution. A comprehensive array of comparable characteristics is listed in the Table 2.

Education all around the world has benefited by importing and incorporating the management concepts from industry. Millcreek Township Public Schools, Pennsylvania, Rappahannock County Public Schools, Virginia; Prince William County Public Schools, Virginia; Southwestern Wisconsin Quality Consortium, Wisconsin and Vermount Department of Education, Vermount are noteworthy in their efforts towards TQE (Konopricki, 1996).

Management Techniques in Education

There are many management techniques that are finding their way to management of education quality. Prominent among them are discussed below:

(a) Deming's 14 Points For Management

The management approach of Edwards Deming has significant implications for the reform of

Table 2. Characteristics of a Quality Institution and an Ordinary Institution

Quality Institution	Ordinary Institution
• Customer centered	• Centered on internal needs
• Focused on preventing problems	• Focused on detecting problems
• Invest in people	• No systematic approach to staff development
• Treat complaints as an opportunity to learn	• Treat complaints as nuisance is vague about standard of quality
• Have well defined quality characteristics for all areas of the organization	• Have no quality plan
• Senior management process involves everybody	• Only the management team is involved
• Have collective performances and responsibility	• Have individual responsibility
• Concurrent performance appraisal	• Retrospective performance appraisal
• Flexible planning	• Rigid planning
• Have egalitarian culture	• Have hierarchical culture
• Plans are long term	• Plans are short term
• Quality is seen as a part of the culture	• Quality is seen as a troublesome initiative

education (Holt, 1993, a). Deming's philosophy and his 14 points for management are finding their way into education. Holt (1993, b) has interpreted Deming's 14 Points for Management in an educational context :

(1) Create constancy of purpose for improvement of product and service

- Establish the moral purpose of the school

(2) Adopt the new philosophy

- Make the transformation to the new philosophy

(3) Cease dependence on mass inspection

- Focus not on outputs but on the activity of teaching and learning

(4) End the practice of awarding business on the basis of price tag

- Examine proposed innovations carefully

(5) Improve constantly the system of production and service

- Identify and solve curriculum problems in the context of the school system

(6) Institute training on the job

- Invest in teachers

(7) Adopt and institute leadership

- Establish collegiality and optimize the system

(8) Drive out fear

- Promote mutual respect and trust

(9) Break down barriers between departments

- Cooperate

(10) Eliminate slogans, exhortations and targets for the work force

- Interrogate the system, not the teachers

(11) Eliminate numerical quotas for the work force

- Minimize objectives and outcomes; focus on educational encounters.

(12) Remove barriers that rob people of pride of workmanship

- No rating of students or teachers.

(13) Encourage education and self-improvement for everyone

- Provide further professional studies

(14) Take action to accomplish the transformation

- Support the programme at all levels, from school board to school.

(b) TQM (Total Quality Mangement) in Education

Education could be benefited from TQM because of the augmented emphasis on quality and customer satisfaction. TQM in education or TQE, Total Quality Education (Hertzke and Olson, 1993) has been tried in many educational institutions (Sallis, 1993; Duden, 1995; Billing, 1996) with impressive results.

Table 3 highlights the difference between TQE and traditional ways of functioning.

(c) CQI (Continuous Quality Improvement)

CQI is a state of mind with some agreed upon values that guide the way in which work is approached (Frazier, 1997). The basic values of CQI are similar to those of TQM or TQE but the "C" indicates continuous process that quality improvement is.

(d) Quality Circles

Quality Circles comprise small groups of 6-8 volunteers from the same work area / department that meet regularly once a week, for an hour to solve their work-related problems. The members receive training in problem solving, statistical quality control and group process. QCs generally recommend solutions for quality and productivity problems that then are implemented by the management. A facilitator, usually a specially trained member helps train Circle members and ensures that things run smoothly (Subramanium etal, 1997).

QCs in Industries

QC, a Japanese concept has been experimented in industries with interesting results. It is a voluntary concept that stimulates a person's creativity and channelises his energies to optimization of his talents.

Florida Power and Light Company, Miami, saved more than $25 millions through 700

Table 3. TQE Challenges In Education

Quality Element	*Traditional School Organisation*	*TQE*
The definition of Quality is....	Result oriented	Child oriented
The decisions are based on....	Short term goals	Balancing short term and long term goals
The emphasis is on.............	Reasons for failure	Prevention of failure
The organisational culture tends towards................	Pointing fingers, blaming and punishing risk takers	Continuous improvement and reward to achievers
The outcome changes from...	Simple learning of subjects	Multi-dimensional development
The executives and heads of departments change from...	Score-keepers	Leaders by personal example
The criterion of merit changes from......	Performance based on stuffing the brains	Developing/training the mind and its abilities
The organisatonal structure of schools	Hierarchical, bureaucratic, and static	Flat, integrated and fluid
Problem solving is by.......	Those in authority, top of pyramid only	Teams, all levels of staff and even students

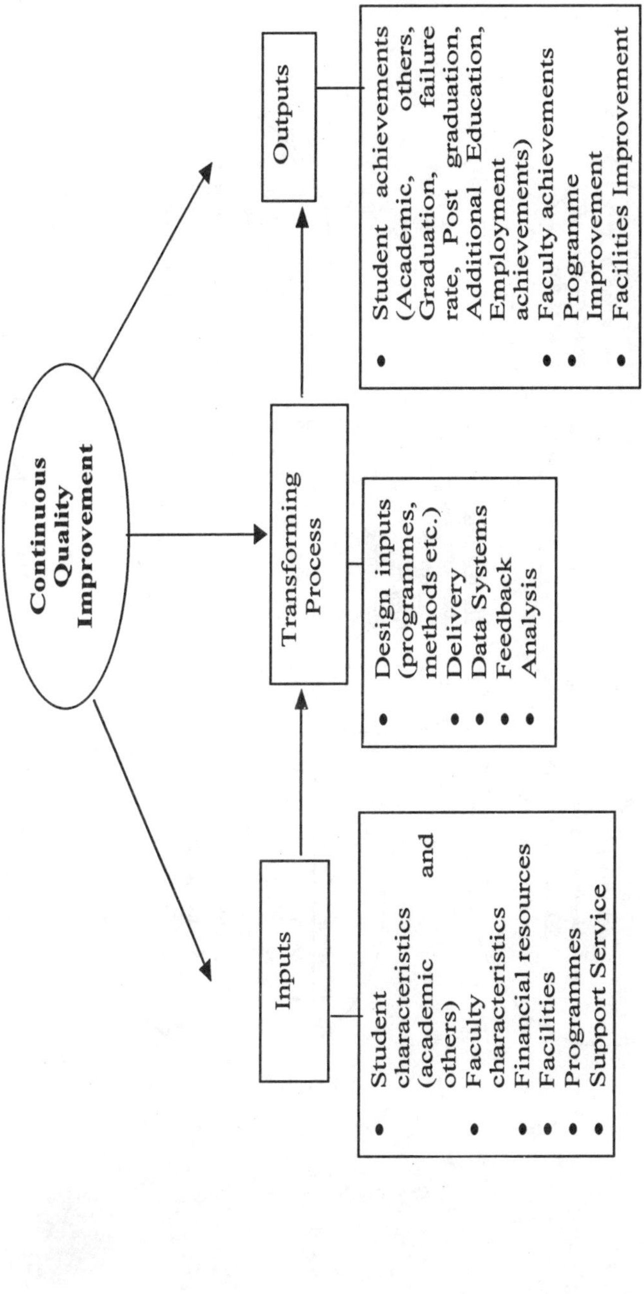

Fig. 1. Integrating Quality Improvement in Higher Education (Lewis and Douglas, 1998)

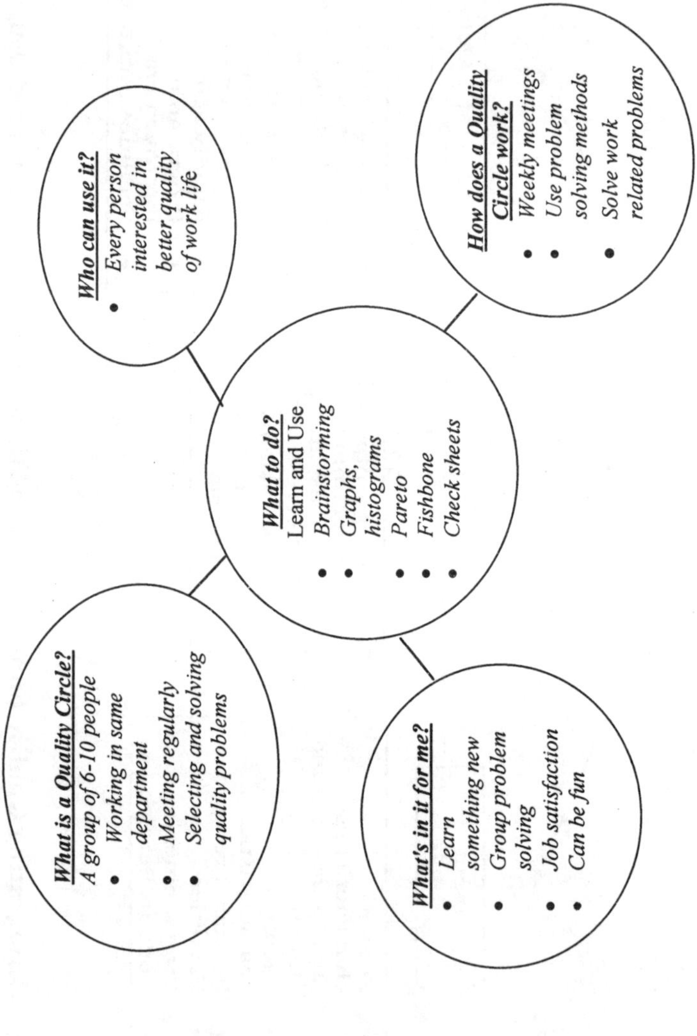

Fig. 2. QCs- What, How And For Whom

documented quality improvement project QCs. Textron, Inc.'s Fafnir Bearing Division in New Britain, Connecticut producer of aerospace ball and roller bearings launched QC programme in early 1981 with 28 people in 4 QCs. Within a year participation grew to 100 workers in 16 QCs on a strictly voluntary basis. The results included increased job satisfaction and dollar savings (Banks, 1989).

In India , at Fag Precision Bearing Ltd., Baroda, since inception in 1994, just eight QCs resulted in increased turnover of around Rs. 5.00 lakhs, greater customer satisfaction, better housekeeping, increase in confidence level of workers and fulfilling organisational needs (Athshere, 1996). Mukand Ltd, Mumbai is working towards QC culture since 1990 and had within five years, 58 QCs functioning in the different sections of the company (Rau, 1995). At Steel Authority of India Limited (SAIL), Bhilai, 10,987 QCs have functioned which is the largest in any public sector undertaking (Khosla, 2000). At Nippon Denro Ispat Ltd., Dolvi, QCs were launched in 1993 in the Sponge Iron production unit. The training imparted due to such activities enabled workers to identify work related problems and come up with recommendations. It also enabled then to achieve some basic needs (Varma, 1996). At Bharat Heavy Electronics Limited (BHEL), Bhopal, a QC called QC117CIM had had 750 meetings and solved 150 problems in 16 years (QC117, 2000).

Many researchers (Robson, 1984; Chandran 1986; Levit 1994; Subramanian 1996; and Dewar,

1999) have found QCs to be beneficial for quality improvement because :

- Everybody participates and contributes in the process of decision-making.
- Problems are chosen, not given.
- Decision by consensus, not by majority.
- Performance oriented, not problem focused.
- Promotes prevention, not inspection.
- Management blessed, not management directed.
- Reinstates the dignity of the worker and helps in building positive attitudes.
- Removes management-worker divides developing commonality of objectives.
- Allows a person to become more involved without putting any pressure.
- Harmonious relations at work place and the organisation gets a total person.
- Humanizes the work, i.e., quality of work life is stressed and improved.
- Brings out extraordinary quality from ordinary people.
- Recognizes and taps the intellectual and creative potential of participants.

Some arguments for and against the efficacy of QCs are listed below in Table 4.

Table 4. Can QCs Work in Education?

QCs will not work, if	QCs will work, when....
QCs are for solving managements' problems	• QCs are for employees' growth and development
QCs in industries are for improving products but education has no products	• Products of education (students) are equally important as industrial products. For the benefit of all, we must have QCs
QCs extract more work from sincere and simple people	• QCs "empower" sincere and simple people
It is too much "talk" and less results.	• If the concept is understood clearly.
It will breed few achievers and dump the rest.	• It converts the average into high achievers who have "built in" rewards and motivate the rest to do their best
Qc's are an endless agony of teams, meetings, seminars and reports.	• It is the highest form of an individual's morphosis, a transition both on the personal frontand at the work place.

Management Concepts in Education - Another Perspective

Quality initiatives borrowed from industry have not been without their critics. Serious doubts are raised regarding the applicability of industrial concepts to education on as-is basis since the goals of the two settings are different.

Taylor (1994) has argued that the teacher-student relationship is much more than a one-way provision of goods and services. Education, he contends, ought not to be planning merely to satisfy the wishes of employers; it should seek to redefine their expectations. Moreover, as Fish (1995) notes, colleges and schools are already subjected to many forms of quality assurance from such bodies as the Higher Education Funding Councils, etc. The imposition of further controls, she contends is both unnecessary and likely to add a further burden to the workload of teachers.

Ghosh, (1990) and Venkataiah, (1999) argues that the package theory of management cannot be extended mutandis -mutandis to education system because:

- The 'customer' of education is different from that of industries. Education's customers are those who receive the end product of education's service (Tomlin, 1994). The students, parents and the society are all education's customers.
- Industry has a different goal and mandate. Its aims are profit oriented whereas educational

institutions primarily deal with human resources. The aims of the two are very different. Industry's motives are profit-oriented whereas the focus in education is development of the potentials of each individual to the utmost.

- Industry is profit making, money oriented organisation whereas education system is for "search of truth" and "knowledge".
- Service conditions and physical environments of both are different. "Hiring and firing" is common in industry, in education it is generally, 'not done'.
- Education involves direct contact between provider and end user unlike in industries. The suppliers to industries do not always play a significant role beyond the supply of raw goods. In education, the suppliers play a very significant role in shaping the "product". The teachers and parents are the suppliers that help in shaping a child's development.
- Industries have an option of mending a bad product but education's "products" cannot be repaired. In education the real product is produced in the classrooms.
- Industries have tangible gains and losses whereas they are intangible in education.

It is imperative to remember that educational institutions in developing cannot follow their counterparts from developed countries in adopting quality enhancement programmes. The quality programmes must be chosen to suit the conditions prevailing in developing countries by being simple in design, modest in expectations and realistic in requirements. Bringing about the transformation that result from the implementation of quality is not just identifying concepts and processes within a business context and looking for their duplications in education, so that they can be reduced to yet another ready-to-use package. Instead, the essential ideas need to be investigated in the context of each individual institute, taking into account the system within which the institution functions.

As Stella and Gyanam (2004) emphasizes every institution should raise questions about its own effectiveness, seek answers, and significantly improve procedures in the light of its findings. The deciding factor in assessing the effectiveness of any institution is evidence of the extent to which it achieves its goals and objectives. Higher educational institutions should assure itself and its stakeholders that its policies, systems and processes for development, maintenance and enhancement of quality in all its educational offerings are functioning effectively.

3
Quality Circles in Education

"The significant problems we face can not be solved with the same thinking that created them".

Albert Einstein

The bottom line of all development is the human factor. Japan owes its success more to the mind-set of its work force than high technology. Many organizations invest heavily in expensive automatons and machinery in the mistaken belief that the recipe for success is high technology and not the attitudes of workers and managers.

The research findings on QCs, although conducted in industrial environments have implications for education. The studies indicate that QCs can 'develop' the human resources and in education the human resources are the most important and accessible resources. So education can benefit tremendously by initiating QCs. The feeling of 'oneness' with the organisation, personality development, sense of fulfillment, positive attitude, and improved creativity are the chief benefits reported in industry which can also be exploited in education. The studies also send cautious signals that when QCs are not initiated in appropriate manner and in right spirit they can produce disheartening results.

Kaplan (1990) also opines that the concept of QCs can come to the rescue of university administration as they are expected to mobilize, organize and maximize human physical and fiscal resources.

Objectives of QCs in Education

"The future society belongs to those who are well educated and well-trained and those who have mastered various advanced skills."

(Fu, 1996)

The concept of QC has come to education from industry. Although the principles of the concept are same in both the set ups, the focus is different in academics. In education the objectives of initiating QCs are:

- To develop a holistic personality.
- To help in self-development, mutual development, organisational development and eventually societal development.
- To infuse a spirit of duty, responsibility and team work.
- To enable people to find the deeper meaning of life and to raise the material and spiritual level of man.

- To build analytical minds so that people have scientific approach to problems.
- To fully reveal human capabilities and eventually draw out infinite possibilities by creating new learning environment.
- To make education more relevant and usable to the internal, external customers.
- To initiate Total Quality Education (TQE).

The traditional education, which had the task of preparing for stereotyped functions and stable situations, for a particular job is outdated and obsolete in modern times. The QC approach gives a new dimension to education sector.

Quality Circles: Genesis

The concept of quality originated in 1920's when Shewart, a physicist at AT & T's Bell laboratory in the U.S. gave birth to the management science called "Quality" by importing statistical concepts from agricultural research into manufacturing system. The fuse of quality revolution was lit when W. Edwards Deming, a disciple of Shewart, introduced a shift of statistical checks from the inspection to the inception stage. Deming's methods were used in his native U.S. in armament production during World War II but were forgotten in the post war buoyancy in the U.S. and European markets that rendered quality a rather irrelevant issue in the eyes of industry.

In Japan, the scene was very different. After the world war – I, Japan became infamous for its shabby

Table 5 : The QC Approach vs The Traditional Approach

Dimension	*QC Approach*	*Traditional Approach*
Teacher's role	Personal, as a friend and guide	Impersonal and distant
Types of objectives to be achieved	Cognitive, emotional and value oriented	Stated and prescribed
Instructional approach	Discovering together and emphasis on learning by doing	One-way, rigid, emphasis on rote learning
Relevance to life	Imparts usable, analytical & practical approach to problem at all fronts	Little
Making a difference	Problem solving in teams, so collective decisions and collective implementation	Each individual is an island. Even if there are good ideas they are not implemented

quality of goods. After the Second World War Japan was totally devastated. Conditions after the war were deplorable for the workers. There was widespread unemployment and underemployment. Japanese Union of Scientists and Engineers (JUSE) headed by Dr. Ishikawa made an attempt to improve the conditions for the workers in 1947 but soon realized that they were not able to make a marked difference.

In 1950 they invited Deming for a four-day seminar, who advocated SQC (Statistical Quality Control) for production department. In 1957-58 Japan declared T.Q.C. (Total Quality Control) as their national policy. By 1960 the conditions for the workmen changed for the better but still only managers, supervisors were involved. For every one-trained person there were 38 untrained. So JUSE thought of starting a magazine called FQC (Fundamentals of Quality) with a minimal cost equivalent to two packets of cigarettes in which workers could ask their doubts. The response they got was overwhelming. They got wagonloads of queries which they could not even open to read leading to the birth of study Circles. Study Circles were formed at the work place itself where one trained person (foreman / supervisor) gave training to other eight untrained workers (Ganapathy et al, 1994). In 1962 when study Circles became problem-solving Circles they were called Quality Circles.

Today more than 80 per cent of Japanese working population is involved in the QC movement with more than 403,848-registered QCs (Amardasa, 1999).

According to Japanese Union of Scientists and Engineers (JUSE), some 5.5 million workers are members of QCs. QCs are applied to both production and non-production areas in Japan (Dale, 1999). Today, JUSE continues to provide over 200 courses per year, including five executive management courses, ten management courses, and a full range of technical training programmes (Cortada and Woods, 1999).

QC is ideological and people-friendly concept. The basic ideas/concepts of QC activities are:

- Respect for humanity and building a happy workplace
- That every person, no matter where in the organisation desires to do quality work
- He/she would like to be respected and would like to contribute to the growth, welfare of the institution
- That the individual on the job has the most knowledge of that particular job
- Teamwork can be more effective and can contribute more than individual effort
- That members must be given opportunity to tap their untapped potentials
- Members' contribution requires recognition
- Training is an integral part to develop the QC movement

In India, in the field of QCs, QCFI (Quality Circle Forum of India) is one of the foremost national organisations promoting quality movement since its birth in 1982. QCFI is a non-profit organisation with its headquarters at Sikandrabad. It has 25 chapters all over the country. It has around 800 corporate and institutional memberships, around 8,000 individual memberships and around 10,000-registered QCs. The focus of QCFI is to empower the grass root level of employees in industry, government organisations, academia, banks, hospitals etc. through QC movement.

Lucknow Education Society, which runs many schools under its aegis, is pioneer in practicing QCs in schools. The City Montessori School (CMS) Degree College, Kanpur road, Lucknow, organizes International Convention of Students' QC (ICSQCC) every two years. Many countries have been participating in the conventions organized in December 1999, 2001, 2003, and 2005. The chief feature of the Convention is to give recognition to SQC (Students' QC). They have also made efforts to institutionalize the concept by establishing the World Council for Total Quality and Excellence in Education with CMS as the corporate office.

Many educational institutes over the world have used the concept of Quality Circles, albeit in various garbs with interesting results. Table 6 shows the achievements of QCs.

Table 6 : QCs in Educational Institutions

Education Institute	QC Achievements
Abroad	
Glenwood, Maryland	Every student works in one or more "S-Teams" (support teams) to learn how their work- individual and collective can be improved (Bonstingl, 1992
Statewide project in the high schools in New Jersey, U.S.A.	Used brain storming sessions and Ishikawa diagram to solve the problem of students' absenteeism. (Sallis, 1993)
Kirrawee High School, Sydney, Australia	"Quest" Quality Circle solved problem of traffic flow at the front of the school. (Diwan, 1995)
George Westinghouse Vocational and Technical High School,	Students and staff together tried to introspect about the lack of quality in schools. The reasons ranged

Table 6 continued......

Education Institute	QC Achievements
New York	from underpaid, lazy, untrained staff; lack of education, singleness, uncommunicative parents' lack of self-respect, undisciplined, peer pressure on the part of students to give less importance to education, emphasis on material goods on the part of society. Together the staff & students attempted to solve the problems. (Schargel, 1995)
Singapore government has promoted a national body called "QC College"	All QC leaders and facilitators have to compulsorily undergo training to be eligible to start QC in their respective organisations whether industrial or educational. (Solbai, 1996)
In India	
Lucknow Education Society, Lucknow U.P.	Has twenty QCs to date. The first ever students' QC, 'Jai-Jagat' presented at 8th International Convention of QCs at Hong Kong in 1993 on "How to concentrate?"

Table 6 continued......

Education Institute	QC Achievements
	(Aggarwal, 1994)
International Convention of Students Quality Circles (ICSQC 1997 and 1999) Lucknow U.P.	Conventions of students' QC invited participants from India, Singapore, Malaysia, Australia, Srilanka, England, U.S.A., Japan, South Africa, Mauritus, Bangladesh, Nepal and Switzerland. The participants made presentations or read papers. Over 1000 delegates attended the conventions.
Indian Institute of Management (IIT) Calcutta, Nagpur University and College of Engineering of Anna University, Madras	These institutes of higher education have formed QC to improve the quality of higher education. (Tulsi, 1998)

Behavioural Aspects of QCs

The philosophy of QCs can be examined in the context of theorie propounded by the behavioural scientists (Hutchins 1985, Dey 1988 & Subramanian et al, 1997).

(a) Herzberg's Theory

According to Herzberg, the stimuli to which an employee responds in his workplace may be classified into two categories- hygiene or maintenance factors and motivators. Hygiene and maintenance factor include working condition, job security, economic factors, social factors etc. The absence of one or more of these usually makes an employee dissatisfied but their presence does not necessarily ensure job satisfaction. The motivators on the other hand, offer job satisfaction. When the job offers scope of innovation, autonomy, participation, growth and recognition, the employee is motivated to give his best. QCs provide for motivators like innovation, autonomy participation, achievement, recognition etc. in the job. So QCs can motivate people and bring out the best in them.

(b) McGregor's Theory

This theory emphasizes that even when the top management is keen to launch QCs, there is no guarantee that these will succeed in the organization. The success of QCs depends a great extent on the kind of beliefs held by the managers and supervisors about their workers. The beliefs can be classified into two categories- Theory X and Theory Y.

Table 7 : Beliefs of Theory 'X' and 'Y'

Theory X	Theory Y
• A worker has no interest in work.	• A worker has internal drive for accomplishment and pride in work manship.
• He is lazy and uncooperative.	• Industry makes his job meaningless and monotonous.
• He is interested only in money.	• It stifles his natural drive and creativity.
• Offer monetary incentives for meeting standards and impose penalties for failure	• Create new job conditions to remove his frustrations.

(c) Maslow's Hierarchy of Needs

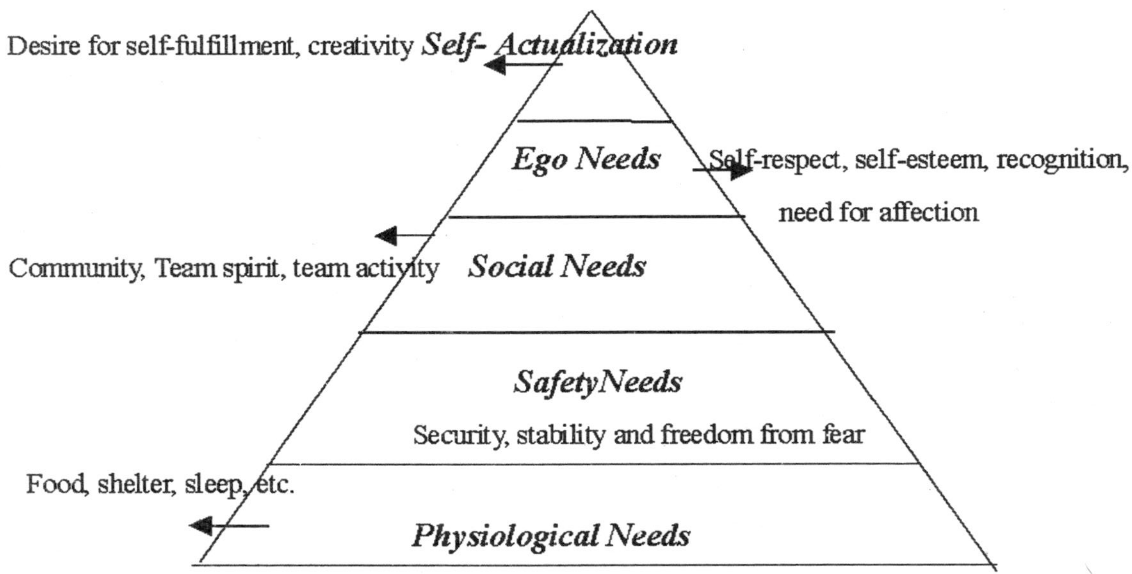

Fig. 3. Maslow's hierarchy of Needs

QCs in the departments of theory Y managers and supervisors are more likely to succeed because they have trust in the intrinsic worth of their workers and they believe that given proper opportunities the workers are capable of making creative and innovative suggestions concerning their jobs and work environment

(c) Maslow's Hierarchy of Needs

Maslow's theory highlights that only when an individual's physiological, safety, social, ego needs are fulfilled will he seek self-actualization. Individuals with reasonably satiated basic needs are more likely to participate in QCs as QCs realises higher order needs.

QC is a forum for the fulfillment of an employee's higher order needs. Although it might be ambitious to claim that every QC member will be able to satisfy his self-actualization needs, surely his social and ego needs are likely to be satisfied provided his QCs function properly and the management pays enough attention to recognise the success of QC members.

QCs – Impact on The Individual

The individual participating in QC activities is benefited as shown in figure 4.

Studies on QCs have reported benefits to the members themselves and the employing organisation. Rafaeli (1985) found that QC members described a feeling of oneness with the organisation and

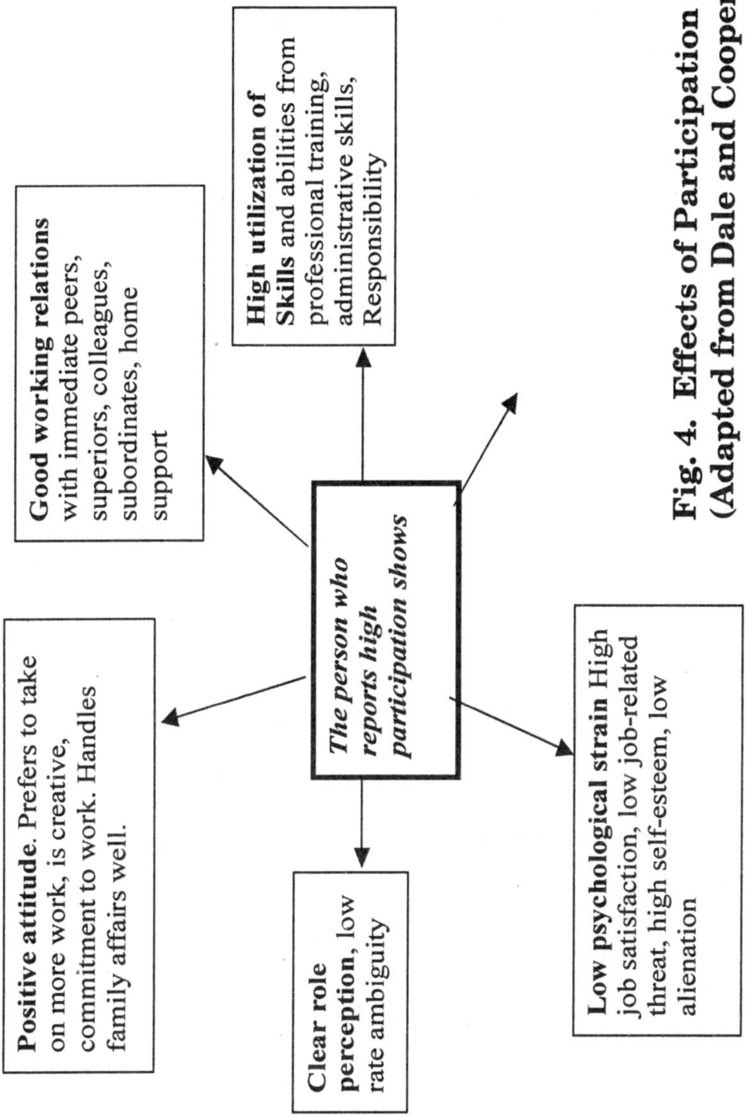

Fig. 4. Effects of Participation in QCs (Adapted from Dale and Cooper, 1997)

significantly few members left the organisation as compared to the non-members. Bradley and Hill, (1987) found that executives involved in QC activities reported that they had come to appreciate more potential intangible benefits such as better human relations resulting from improved communication.

Jayavelu et al (1994) conducted a survey of 186 individuals who represented the QC teams of different organisations throughout the country. They found that QC participation helps in personality development, recognition of self worth and brings about a sense of fulfillment.

A large Indian public sector organisation involving 50 QC leaders among service department and manufacturing department was surveyed (Thakur and Nagar, 1999). The results revealed that the respondents rated their QCs as more effective and rated the prospect of QCs as bright. The members felt that the issue of attitudinal change is most important to revitalise dormant QCs. They felt that QC members exhibit a more positive approach towards their colleagues, towards other departments and towards their organisation as compared to their counterparts. In the long run, because of attitudinal changes, the QC members exhibit a more positive approach towards their organization as compared to their counterparts.

Srinivasan (1991) carried out a status report on the QC movement in India in which he collected data from public enterprises, private sectors, banks, hospitals, Indian railways and state transport corporations. He found-

- Organizations with QCs had higher levels of operating incomes and gross profit than those not having QCs.
- Compared to hospitals and road transport corporations QCs were functioning much better in banks and railways.
- QCs did not exhibit any perceptible relationship with the average age of the employees and the average size of the organizations.
- The attitude of the major trade unions did not show hostility to the QC functioning. Maheshwari (1987) also reports that a study of 1886 QCs in select Indian companies indicated that the attitude of the unions was positive towards the QC concept. The union members liked the concept because of its voluntary nature. It was also found that non-members were indifferent but not resentful to the QC concept.

The QC Structure

The structure of QCs mainly constitutes the members, facilitators, steering committee, top management and non-members. The members form QCs with the assistance of facilitators and support of top management. They make presentations in front of the steering committee. Usually in an Institution, the number of non-members is more than that of the members.

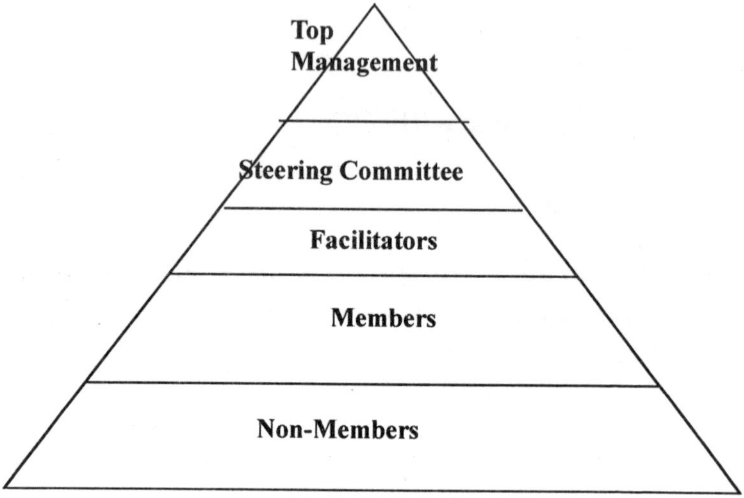

Fig. 5 The QC Structure.

The typical structure of the QCs is shown in the figure 5. It depicts the various committees/bodies in an educational institution when QCs are formed only among the students. When teachers/non teaching staff also forms QCs among them then, "members" and "non-members" will change accordingly.

Individuals from organisations willing to initiate QCs are exposed to an orientation programme which is generally arranged by an outside faculty, Subsequently interested members are encouraged to form QCs. Six to eight volunteers from the same work area are encouraged to form a QC. These volunteers are further exposed to a training programme regarding the functioning of QCs. Within the QCs a leader is chosen by consensus.

Also, a Steering Committee, which is a decision taking committee, is formed consisting of selected members of management and senior staff. Facilitators / coordinators are senior staff with knowledge of QC concept. They help in the smooth functioning of QCs. The top management as part of the Steering Committee selects members of management who show interest in QC concept. The work is delegated according to their aptitude and capabilities. The facilitator normally reports to the Steering Committee.

The Steering Committee is Responsible for:

- Preparation of objectives for the need of QCs in accordance with the institutional philosophy
- To meet regularly with coordinators and guides them
- To identify training needs and promote QC throughout the institution
- To plan launching of QC in every department of the institution
- To provide facilities for QC activities
- To prepare budgets and obtain necessary sanctions for allocation of funds for various QC related activities
- To review training and programme materials
- Update and makes training materials interesting for the members
- To follow up the completed projects
- To give credit to QC teams where due, and organize periodic QC conventions

To initiate QCs in an educational institution, it is firstly, essential to ensure the total commitment of top-level management before starting. Then discussions within the institution with the heads, teachers, administrative staff, unions should be carried out to take them in confidence about your intents and actions. Only then, a facilitator from outside should be called for guidance to implementing the QC programme. QCs can be introduced in an educational institution according to the following steps-

- Appreciation programme for Principals and Teaching staff (Formation of Steering Committee)
- Appreciation programme for Students' Union members (Results in greater awareness)
- Training on tools for students and staff (Formation of facilitators/ coordinators)
- Formation of experimental Quality Circle
- Experimental QC's presentation to the Steering Committee
- Propagation of QCs through out the institution.

Functioning of Quality Circles

The first step in all QC activities is the training of the members. Professionals in the field, impart the training regarding the skills of organized problem solving. During the QC process, each problem passes through the following stages:

(1) **Problem Collection:** The members create a problem bank by collecting the various problems they face during the course of their work. For each problem the members give a priority number depending upon the criteria evolved by them, such as urgency, need, etc.

(2) **Problem Selection:** One of the first tasks of a Circle is to determine the problem they want to solve. The Circle may list as many problems as they can and then rate them. The problem getting the highest rating is chosen. Sometimes the problem with higher ratings may be difficult to solve, may take a longer time to solve, involves factors beyond the control of Circle members etc. It is advisable to initially choose a problem that can show quick results, so that the motivation level of the group remains high.

(3) **Problem Analysis:** Every problem has an effect and underlying causes. The QC members first establish the cause-effect relationships using the brainstorming technique and drawing up an Ishikawa or Cause-effect diagram. To analyse a problem properly and find the correct solutions it is absolutely necessary to establish the facts for which the QC tools like Check sheets, control charts, Histograms, etc. are used.

(4) **Problem Solution:** In an environment conducive to problem solving and group thinking combined with expertise in work area. Various alternative solutions to a problem are put forth

and explored to find the optimum solution, i.e., one, which is workable, feasible and gives maximum benefits.

(5) **Management Presentations:** After selection of a problem, data collection and analyses the recommendations are presented to the management. These presentations are known as QC presentations and have to be made before the management for acceptance of recommendations or sometimes in front of other QC members and non-members for motivating them.

(6) **Implementation, Review and follow-up:** Once the management gives its approval, the QC members draw up a schedule for the implementation of the proposals etc. They also review the results obtained from the projects periodically and take follow-up action if required. (Robson, 1982; Hutchins, 1985; Chandran, 1986; Dey, 1988 and Udpa, 1994)-

The tools used in QC functioning as proposed by Ishikawa are (Terninko, 1999)- Histograms, Scatter diagram, Stratification, Pareto analysis, Check sheets, Cause and Effect diagrams and Control charts.

QCs: The Fundamental Issues

(a) Management's Role

Management commitment to successful QC implementation is as important as water is to fish! Without the top management's genuine commitment, the failure of the QCs is certain and inevitable. The

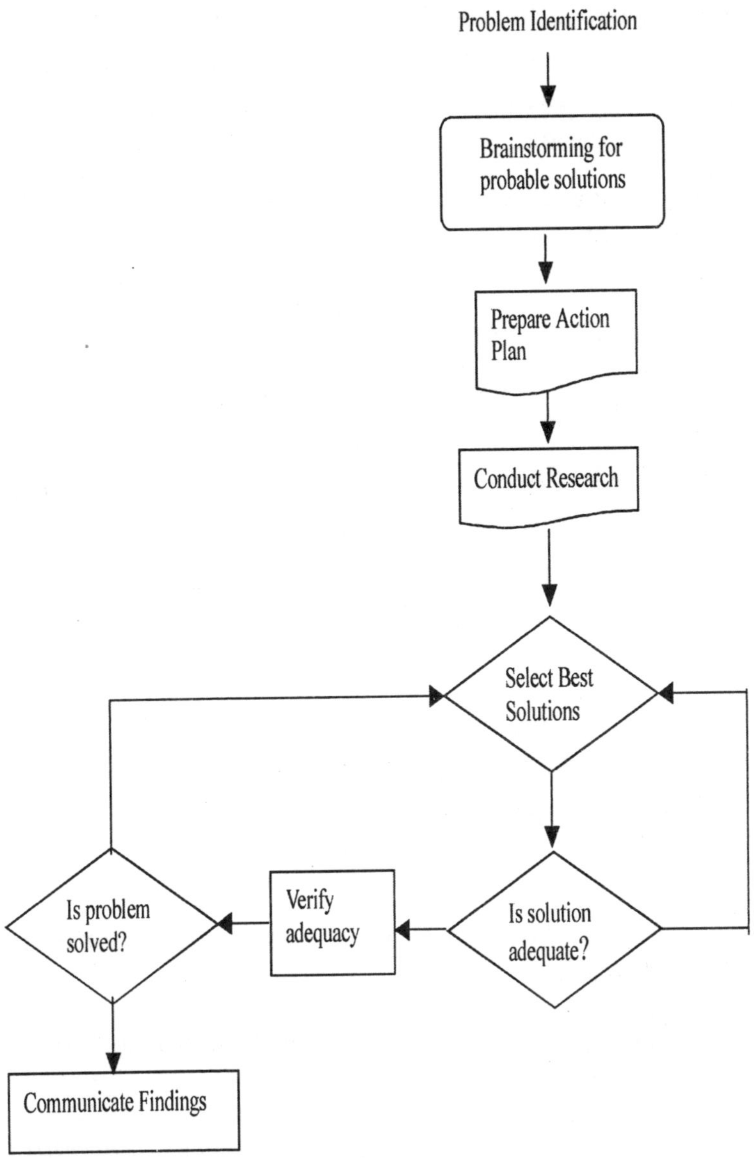
Problem Identification
Brainstorming for probable solutions
Prepare Action Plan
Conduct Research
Select Best Solutions
Is solution adequate?
Verify adequacy
Is problem solved?
Communicate Findings

management must do some serious introspection before starting the QC programme. However, such actions are indicators that all is not well and inquiries should be made to understand the real cause. It should ponder on the following questions and then only take a final decision.

- To what extent it values commitment to the development of the individuals within the system?
- To what extent it values the "we" spirit?
- To what extent it values employees as important members of the organisation?
- To what extent it believes that employees act in the best interest of organisation?
- To what extent it values investing in the development of staff and students?
- To what extent it believes in hierarchy and a feeling that "others" must do their job?
- To what extent it differs in "what it believes" and "what it practices"?

It must be remembered that QCs are NOT:

- A forum for grievances or a springboard for more demands
- A means for the management to off-load their problem
- A tool to change the existing organisational hierarchy
- A forum to criticise individuals or department

- A platform to improve others. QCs are for self-improvement, so the problems undertaken are those that the Circle members face and can be solved by changing selves or immediate environment.

(b) Facilitator's Role

QC members with the facilitator and leader meet regularly once a week, for an hour to solve quality related problems. The involvement in the QC is strictly on a voluntary basis. The members solve work-related problems and convey the developments to the facilitator / coordinator. The facilitator / coordinator encourages them to make a presentation in front of selected members of the management i.e., the Steering Committee, that may or may not accept the recommendations. The Steering Committee passes the recommendations to the top management and steps are taken to implement the recommendations.

A facilitator is the one who facilitates the process of Quality Circle activities. He should have the skill in communicating effectively, perseverance and amiable temperament.

The Functions of a Facilitator are:

- To ensure that QCs comply with the guidelines laid down by the Steering Committee

- To participate as an active member of the Steering Committee and act as a link between the Steering Committee and different QCs of the institution

- To train members, leaders, and act as a link between different QCs
- Arrange and attend Circle meetings and maintain Circle records
- Organizes informal gatherings – invites speakers
- Searches for new ideas and solve personal problems
- Publicise the concept of QC and motivates non-members to join the movement
- To forward and recommend results/ solutions to the Steering Committee
- Helps in preparing for presentations, invitation, papers, visual aids
- Follows up on completed projects

The facilitator must know of all the developments in the QCs. As he is the link between the workforce (QCs) and management, he should at least be informed of all developments.

(c) Leader's Role

The QC leader is one who directs the QC activities towards conclusion for results. The QC leader is a unanimously chosen member of the QC. His selection is not based on his designation but on his personal traits like leadership qualities, enthusiasm, popularity etc. After completion of one project some other member can become the leader so that every QC member can get a chance to develop leadership skills.

Functions of a QC leader-

- To generate enthusiasm for Circle activities in his/her department
- Delegate work systematically and take care of Circle's operations
- Meet with the Circle once a week
- Use facilitator for assistance and present results/ solutions to Steering Committee
- Be responsible for Circle's periodic review reports and progress records
- Creates harmony and coordination in the Circle
- Work closely with seniors and be a key link between management and members
- Enforce code of conduct and keep the meeting on track

(d) Members's Role

QC members are not selected but are volunteers. If more people wish to join a QC than can be accommodated, the alternatives of forming more than one Circle or to reduce the number by some form of lottery should be considered. It is more important to ensure that all QC members and non-members are aware that they all will have the opportunity to become involved in QC activities, if they wish.

Functions of QC Members

- Attend meetings on time and follow the code of conduct

- Readiness to put in extra hours of work for QC activities
- To learn statistical techniques and contribute to problem-solving
- Promote QC programmes and share information with fellow members
- Motivate new members to join
- Participate in presentations on QCs

(e) Problem Solving

Problem solving can be divided into two stages :
(1) Data Collection (2) Data Analyses

(1) Data Collection

1. **Check Sheet.** It is a format for documentation/ presentation of relevant data in an appropriate and elegant manner. Data collected thus, scientifically brings out the facts thereby eliminating personal bias. Check sheets may be prepared in the following way

(a) *Check Diagrams.* Drawings or pictorial views can be employed, preferably among the lower age children Circle members. It marks the location of defects/complaints to find out problem areas.

(b) *Check List*. A list can be made to make sure that all of the critical items are checked. It can be used in the future. It is necessary that the student members understand the use and need of the

good paper work. Check sheet should be simple and useful.

2. **Histograms and Graphs.** Histogram is a form of column graph, which displays distribution of values obtained whenever numerical data is collected. Here the values of a continuous distribution are represented by the horizontal axis, which is divided into classes of equal size. Generally, there is one column for each class and the height of that column represents the number of occurrences of data values in the range represented by the class.

Graphs. Graphs are a system of connections or inter-relations among two or more signified by a number of distinctive dots, lines or bars that tells a story without any further explanation. There are many types of graphs used as shown below. It is suggested that these graphs be well explained to QC members for representing the information/data the Circle has collected for its analysis.

(a) **Pie Graphs** are used to show where and what percentage an incident has occurred. The different components of an item are shown in the form of a segment of a Circle. The size of segment represents the percentage, the total being 360 degree. The Pie Graphs are very popular as it is the pictorial representation of data and is enjoyable to make.

(b) **Line Graphs** are the most common of all graphs. They are used to plot things as they happen.

(c) **Bar Graphs** are just like column graphs except that they run horizontally.

(d) **Column Graphs** are just what the name implies and, the vertical column shows the information desired. It is very similar to a histogram.

3. **Control Charts.** Control Charts provide the user with an indication of stability in the process. It is not recommended for QCs of school level.

4. **Sampling.** Drawing out of a small group, representative of the larger group of subjects to be studied is sampling. Sampling saves time and cost while giving representative information about the sample to be studied.

(a) *Random Sampling.* All parts of the data are treated equally and then samples are chosen for evaluation. The procedure of selection could be use of random numbers from tables or odd/ even numbers e.t.c.

(b) *Stratified Sampling.* It involves dividing the data into two or more groups so that each group can be evaluated separately. Sorting the data thus helps to pinpoint problem areas.

Data Analyses Techniques

1. Brainstorming

It is a technique for generating a large number of solutions in a short space of time, collectively. The underlying principle is that people in groups are able to generate more and better ideas than as individuals. In QCs it is used to identify problems in the first place, analyse causes and for producing ideas for possible solutions. Also, it is used in a variety of other situations when it is appropriate. It is a powerful technique and when done well can be great fun.

2. Pareto Diagram

Pareto Analysis is based on the Pareto principle proposed by Vil Fredo in the 1940's, who had observed that about 80% of the national wealth belonged to about 20% of population. This "80-20" principle or the principle of "vital few and trivial many or useful many" has its ramifications in various fields. In QCs problem solving, this technique is used to make the "vital few" and "trivial many" causes obvious to the observer, to create criteria for the next step i.e. generating ideas for problem solution and to practice convergent thinking. . It is a special bar or column graph. The diagram represents data arranged in descending order from left to right. A cumulative line if used represents the sum of the groups added together.

3. Cause and Effect Diagram

It is named after Ishikawa of the University of Tokyo who first developed it in 1943. It is also called a fish bone diagram because it resembles the skeleton of a fish. It is a very useful technique for the identification of the causes and sub-causes of the problems. It is an organised method of gathering and recording causes of problem. It helps to minimise uncertainties. The Cause and Effect diagram has found immense use among Quality Circles. It has been observed that most of the problems can be treated as effects of different causative forces which can be

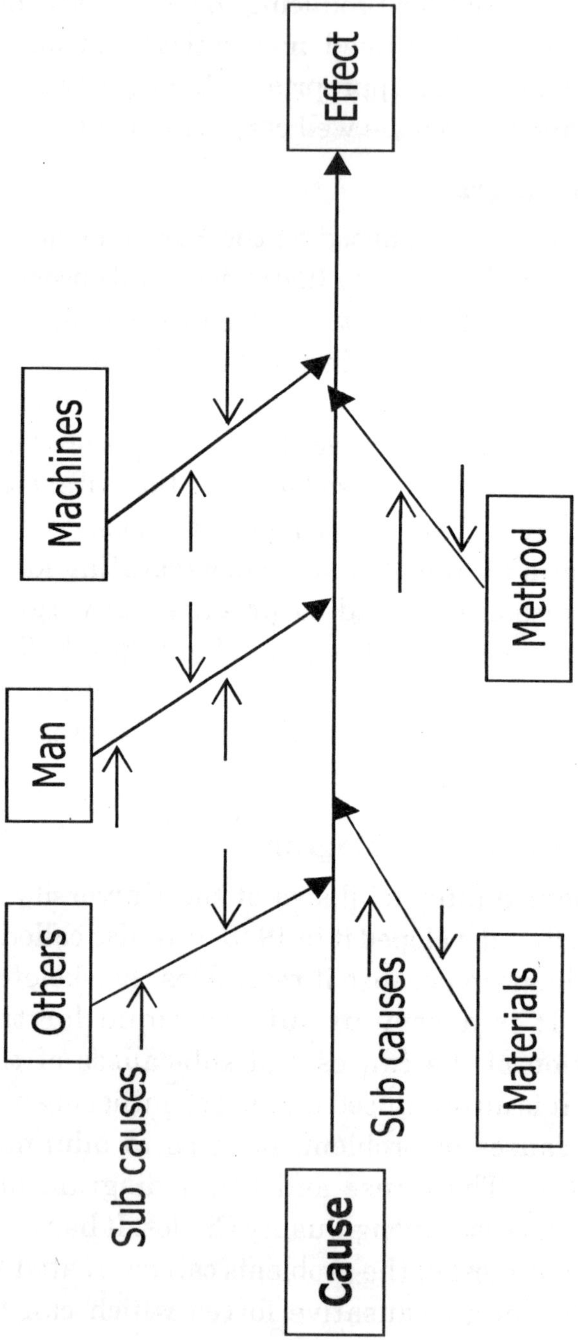

Fig. 6 Fish Bone Diagram

categorised under 5"M's- (i) Man (ii) Machine (iii) Materials (iv) Methods and (v) Miscellaneous/others.

QCs: A Word of Caution

Although the benefits of QCs are well documented, QCs in the classical sense have not been too "successful" in the western organisations. One reason cited is because they were introduced at a time in the west when organisations did not fully understand and practice the principles of TQM (Dale, 1999).

In India QCs were at peak in 1980's but after 1992 there was a decline. Today efforts are underway to revive the concept in Indian organisations (Rao, 2000). QCs failed because management tried to put the blame for their failures also on QCs (Dhantingan, 2000).

Other *reasons for QC failure* cited are (Hutchins, 1985; Udpa 1994 and Jaycox, 1996)-

- Resistance to a new concept (a Japanese concept not suiting Indian milieu)
- Lack of management support
- A fear of loss of authority by the management.
- Members may feel "used" and mistrust the management
- No time and an overwhelming workload
- Skepticism among employees; workers with personal grievances.
- Not a team player and a "I don't care" attitude

- A low self-esteem, a belief that my ideas are not so important
- Selection of QC members, leaders and problems by management
- Short term objectives; emphasis on faster results
- Incompetent QC leadership and Lack of supportive facilities

Fabi (1992) analysed forty empirical studies undertaken on QCs. From examination of his work he identified several factors which are critical to the success of QCs. Salient among them are- management commitment and support, involvement and support of employees and unions, personal characteristics of the facilitator, individual characteristics of members and organization readiness and implementation. Ingle, (1985); Dey, (1988) and Chandra and Janakiram, (1992) have suggested *indicators to make QCs work.*

- Right, conducive conditions for acceptance of the concept
- Preparation for unforeseen risks appropriate publicity
- Avoidance of too much paper work
- Support for QCs from the top management
- Competent middle management and committed, receptive and cooperative workers
- Availability of technical literature and relevant data.

- Financial assistance and availability of training facilities

Studies have indicated that if QCs are initiated either for "wrong" reasons or in "wrong" ways then they are unlikely to be successful. Goodfellow, (1981) studied Twenty-nine American companies with QC and found that only eight companies were successful. The main thrust of the training programme in successful companies was not only on technical concepts but also on the supervisory tools that could be used to motivate the employees.

Bartlett, (1985) studied twenty-five British companies involved with QCs and found that eleven of these were doing quite well and the number of QCs in each had grown substantially. Six others had just 2-3 QCs and remaining eight had already ceased to operate the Circles. It was found that out of 8 where QCs failed, 6 did not have trained leaders and in 4 the sole objective of forming QCs was short-term cost saving. Udpa (1986) reports that only 40 per cent of the organizations having QCs can claim to have all the 100% of QCs working actively.

Dey (1999) reports the findings of a survey of 158 organizations registered with the QCFI as:-

- The success/failure of QC experiment are in no way related to the type of organization.
- 56 per cent of the organizations reported the QC experiment as successful, 12 per cent as a failure and 32 per cent did not have a clear opinion either way.

- Top management support and acceptance by middle and junior management were the most important factors contributing to the success of QCs in Indian organization.
- On the other hand, lack of cooperation from the middle and first line of management was primarily responsible for their failure.

Lal, (1994) suggests that while initiating QCs in Indian milieu, care should be taken to *Adapt* and definitely not *Adopt* the entire Japanese programme. Only those features need be adopted which are feasible and can operate smoothly while modifying others. She suggests temporarily abandoning the voluntary nature of the QC. She recommends that as soon as an employee joins an organisation, human resource department should make him familiar with QC concepts and impart training under the guidance of competent authorities.

QCs can contribute to the "efficient and inexpensive provision of high-quality goods and services, the attainment of greater respect for humanity and the building of worthwhile lives, enhanced human abilities and the creation of an affluent, humanistic and peaceful society for all people, everywhere" (Ishikawa, 1984). QCs or for that matter any quality improvement endeavours can only succeed in an environment of mutual trust, faith, dynamic leadership and a zeal to undertake quality initiatives on continuous basis.

4
The Emergent Paradigm

"Education is not to teach men facts, theories or laws, not to reform or amuse them or make them expert technicians. It is to unsettle their minds, widen their horizons, inflame their intellect, teach them to think straight, if possible, but to think nevertheless"

Robert Maynard Hutchins

Life in the coming decades in educational institutions at all levels is likely to bring new strains together with unprecedented possibilities. To enable the people to benefit in the new environment will require new designs of human resource development. Many of the strategies of quality improvement in education are derived from industrial setting. Challenges to the adoption and implementation of management concepts in educational institutions are several. One has to overcome the challenges to be able to take the best from industrial experiences and combine this, in a holistic framework, with the methods more suited to the educational-milieu. The Challenges are:-

The Rejection of Industrial Models and Vocabulary

The occupational culture of education has in the past been an anti-industry, anti-management, anti-measurement and "anti-pursuit of effectiveness" posture (Morgan and Murgatroyd, 1994). Certain vocabularies like "performance, product, customer, and measurement" are perceived by many as industrial or commercial terms irrelevant to the educational world and the learning process. Such a value posture arises because quality is understood in the context of its industrial origins and connections.

Quality perspective focuses on the customer or user's point of view- whether staff, student or member of the public. It is a commitment to continuous monitoring of quality improvement and enhanced performance. Education professionals should not deliberate whether students are customers or products. Instead, they should learn how concepts that improve efficiency in industry could be used in education. If the industrial origins of these terms are ignored, this is precisely what everybody concerned with quality improvement in education strives for!

A Tradition of Individualist Rather Than Collectivist Responsibility

Classrooms are viewed as islands of professional autonomy with the processes of teaching and learning too mystic and complex to be the subject of quality management scrutiny. Yet it is acknowledged (George, 1993 and Devi, 1996) that what ails the Indian education most today is the classroom atmosphere-overcrowding, poor attendance, high drop-out and failure rates, content-related teaching.

Teaching and learning quality processes require a significant degree of interaction among academic staff. Good teaching does not stem only from individual performance. Quality system requires leadership, well-designed processes, diligent follow-up and continuous improvement. Quality initiatives are not an infringement on teacher's autonomy in the classroom; instead it is assistance for better teaching and better classroom atmosphere.

"Are We Are Doing Very Well As We Are, Given Under The Present Circumstances?"

Cultures are essentially conservative and homeostasis is the norm. Most people resist changes and are comfortable with what they know (Venkataiah, 1999). Hence the refuge in the question "what's wrong with what prevails now?"

The quality perspective calls for improvement beyond comfort levels of achievement, and argues that the continuing search for quality explores the goals that may appear unattainable in comparison with previous standards. Quality perspective exhorts individuals to be unreasonable and then urges them to achieve the unreasonable levels!

A Tradition of Management by Centralized Decision-Making.

For too long "autocratic" leadership where the

principal takes all the decisions and others follow has governed educational institutions.

Quality initiatives like Quality Circles recognize that the principal is human too and can make mistakes and the best way for the progress of an institution is when everybody is concerned about quality. The staff contributes to the decision making process and hence will understand the problems and reasons of a particular stand. QCs empower people to make decisions and solve problems.

A Myopic View v/s Wider View

Traditionally, the teachers are attached to and concerned only about their subject or their pupils at the expense of a broader view. The restricted approach limits the thinking to a particular class or a particular set of students.

Quality approach, on the other hand takes a broader view of improvement. It focuses on the need to not only improve a certain section of education's stakeholders but to bring about changes impacting the entire community of education.

Implementing Quality Measures Will Kill The Spontaneity in the Classroom.

Spontaneity and creativity add life to teaching and quality is not about measuring everything. Quality is not about measuring or quantifying, it is about planning, visualizing and creativity. "Quality" involves much more than just what can be measured and counted. As Deming (1986) commented 'most

Traditional Management Approach

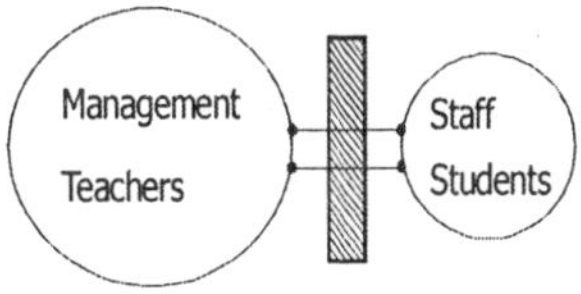

BARRIER WALL

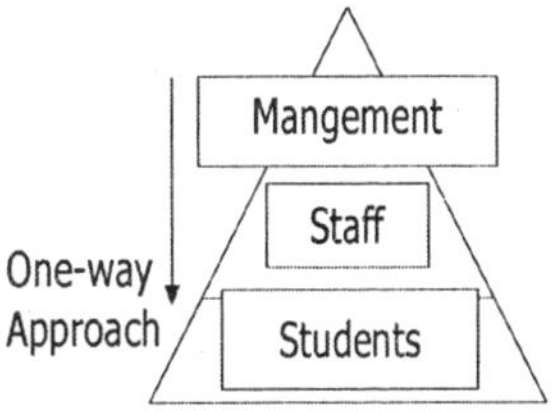

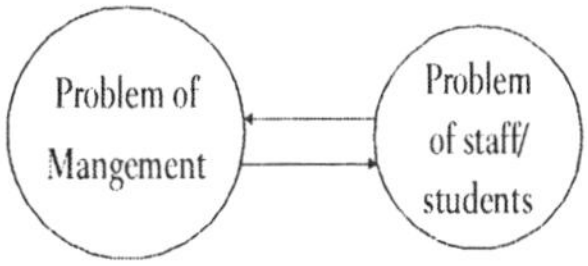

QC Approach

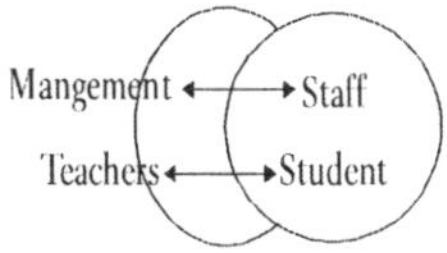

(Congruence of goals established Walls of mistrust broken)

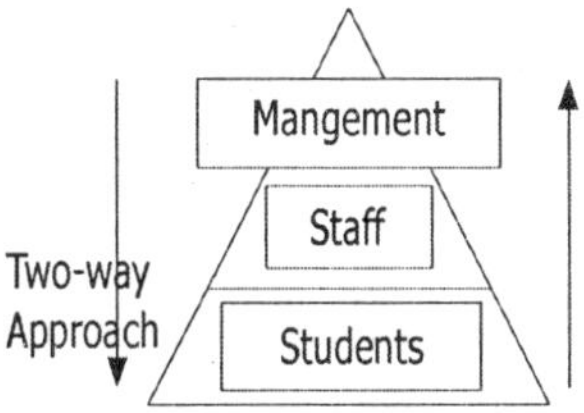

Together the management/staff/ students find solutions for their problems important gains cannot be measured, only the easy ones'.

At A Very Basic Level People Cannot Change

The general perception that it is very difficult to bring about basic attitudinal changes in people is based on the tendency to expect too much, too soon.

The key attributes of Quality management strategies like the Quality Circles as a change agent in effecting an attitudinal transformation rely on objectivity, respect for another's point of view, teamwork, the ability to revise or modify one's viewpoint when factual evidence points in that direction.

TQE through QCs - A Model

On the basis of the researchers' participation in monitoring, initiating and working with QCCs in educational institutions for over six years, the model, *TQE Through QCs* (Sharma and Kamath, 2002) is suggested.

The need for an education-based model arose because the existing literature is industry oriented / focused. It seems wise to take the best from industrial experiences and combine this, in a holistic framework, with the methods more suited to the educational-milieu. The result could be a captivating crossbred that is uniform yet allows for variation from institution to institution.

Prior to initiation of QCs in an educational institution the institution needs to develop conducive environment for it must be recognized that while it is every body's job in the institution, it will become nobody's job unless the institution's quality process is correctly structured to support both the quality work of individuals as well as the quality teamwork among departments. It must be asked whether the institution has well articulated written mission, vision and policy statements pertaining to quality? Does the institution's motivational environment- its intrinsic and extrinsic reward structure- further improvement of teaching and learning quality?

Once the institution goals are made known to all in the institution, it should move in the direction of implementation, educating staff, training them, creating an environment that supports the policy, providing support systems and all that would help in meeting the requirements of quality.

The initiation of QCs necessitates four phases.

Phases of QCs

1. *Awareness Phase*. Quality Circles is a deceptively simple concept. It is not just getting groups of workers together and giving them some problems to discuss! A major company took five years to get to the point where it understood the concept and where the concept was working optimally (Robson, 1982). Orientation programme for students/ staff/ management on the basic concepts of quality can be conducted. These could be reinforced through the creative expression of the students through debates, essays, story writing, etc.

2. *Commitment Phase.* Intensified awareness across all sections of the institution. This phase also identifies areas for improvement by introspection and brainstorming and by applying the concepts of quality improvement individually and collectively for corrective action plans. The first step in creating conducive environment is that the management understands, knows and is committed towards all quality initiatives.
3. *Education and Involvement.* Active involvement of the entire institution. Problems are identified and solutions attempted through teamwork and fact based decisions. Parents are involved either as audience or as resource persons.
4. *Implementation.* Quality has to be "built in" rather than "inspected at the end". Every endeavour that the institution undertakes reflects its emphasis on quality. The 'implementation' of quality is an on going, continuous process supplemented with insight and future vision.

The suggested model, TQE through QCs (Fig. 7) comprises of three levels, viz. - level I, II and III.

Level I

At this level QCs are initiated among students. Students and teachers are exposed to QC orientation programmes and later on encouraged to form QCs. In the orientation programme the staff, students and even parents are apprised of the management's aim of providing quality education and helping each individual student to realise his potential.

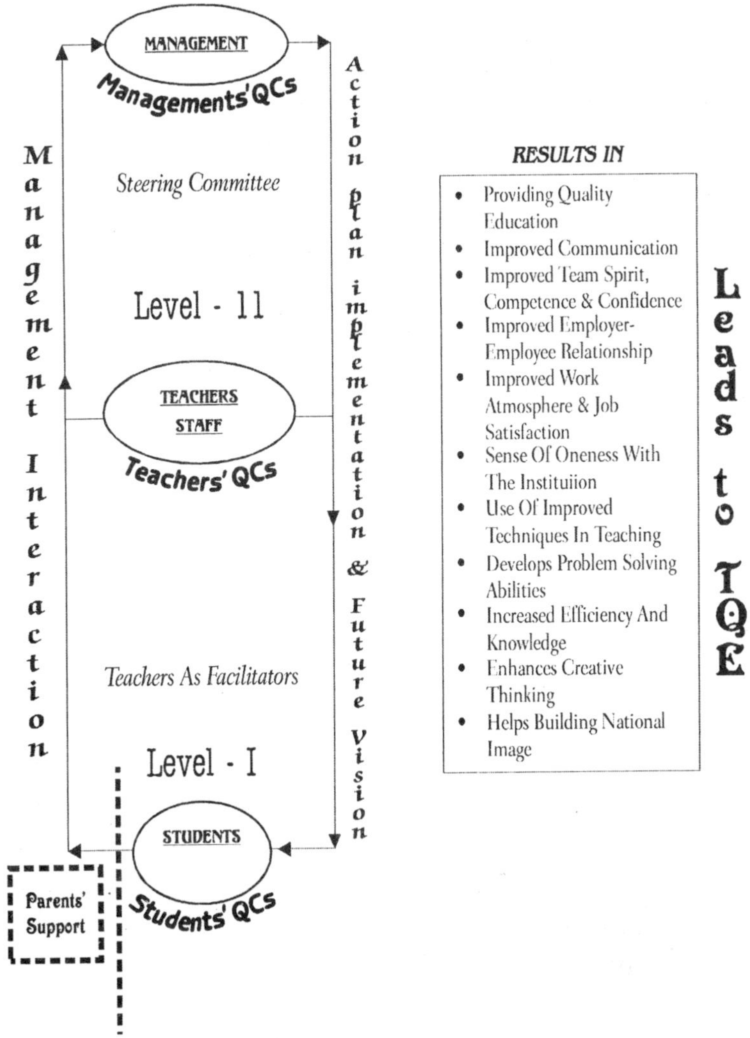

Fig. 7. TQE through QCs

The students' QCs are nurtured by the teachers who act as facilitators. The teacher's role at this level is to guide the students and monitor the development of their QCs. Assistance from the outside faculty is essential here.

Parents also play an important role at this level. They could be invited as resource people for some special QC problem solving or invited as audience to witness the changes in their wards due to QC participation. The parents and parents' association can also help in the QC programme by encouraging and helping the child to fully participate in QC activities. The success of the QC programme depends on the working together of parents, students, teachers and staff together to evolve beliefs, vision, mission and quality standards of educational institutions.

Level II

At level-II, the teachers constitute the QC members. QCs are formed among the teachers.

After making the commitment and real objectives of the management clear in initiating QCs, the teachers are exposed to an orientation programme of QCs. Interested teachers are given further training in QC techniques and QCs are initiated among the teachers. Teachers form a link between students and management with close involvement and deeper insights with both groups.

Direct communication/interaction with the management exists during QC presentations in front of steering committee. Teachers are also in direct communication with students in classroom and in QC meetings

Level III

Level-III constitutes the management's QCs. Although the managements' role is important at levels I & II, it is more visible at level III. At this level, the management members can have their own QC(s) and also a special QC could be formed between managements' representatives, teachers' representatives and students' representatives. This special QC, which is a departure from the accepted norm of having a homogenous group in a QC, can play an important role in improving communication and bridging gaps between the management, teachers and students. It also assists in implementing taken decisions.

If QCs are practiced at all three levels, the results will be as shown in the figure leading to total quality education. However, initially an institution could choose to initiate QCs at any one level and than slowly progress to cover the other levels. It is imperative to keep in mind that the number of QCs initiated are far less important than number of QCs functioning effectively. Dey (1998) concludes that even when the departmental environment is conducive to QCs, not more than 3-4 QCs should be attempted experimentally at the initial stage. These experimental QCs should be nurtured with utmost care so that they do not fail. It is extremely difficult to revive a QC experiment once it has failed at the initial stage.

If any institution chooses to only focus on initiating and continuing QCs at any one level, although it can do so but it would limit the accomplishments of QCs.

Managements' role in the suggested model is of utmost importance. At any level, the management first has to make its objectives, reasons and commitment of initiating QCs very clear. If the managements' commitment is genuine, the chances of the programmes success are enhanced.

As depicted in Fig.7, the management is in direct communication through the steering committee with the students and teachers' QCs. It monitors and notes the growth of QCs in the institution. Also, it creates conducive environment and provides for needed facilities for implementation of action plans. The most important role of the management is in "future vision". The management has to think ahead and plan for the future. It decides on policies, which will result in better and improved quality education in future. In this, it can take help from professionals from India and abroad. It is obligatory to remember, "quality is determined by the top management. It can not be delegated" (Deming, 1997).

The Components of The Model

(a) The Outside Faculty

An experienced faculty can help by giving expertise and an outsider's objective view to the problems. A good training faculty will train the members to run their own programme rather than come in and do it for them. Later on he can visit off and on to monitor the QC programme.

However, it must be remembered that outside experts can teach useful tools and offer encouragement, but they cannot do the work of transformation. A 'yearning for learning' comes ultimately from within the organisation (Bonstingl, 1992)

(b) Role of the QC constituents

Although the roles of QC Members, Facilitators, and Steering Committee are well defined, it is important to keep the human touch intact. Keen and competent facilitators and committed, receptive and fairly literate staff can make QC programme a big success. The parents, teachers, administrators and students will have their roles but they must also share a feeling of oneness with the institution and NOT feel "used". This can be achieved only when there is transparency and truthfulness from the managements' side. The QC constituents must be given a lot of freedom within the constraints of the QC programme.

(c) QC Monitoring

Once the QC programme takes off, it is the management's obligation, with the assistance of outside faculty to keep up the energy levels. The top management -

- Assures that in case of clash between quality and schedule or quality and cost or quality and quantity, quality considerations will receive priority.

- Ensures that it create necessary environment and support systems to enable all employees to implement the policies.

- Has an attitude that aims at prevention of errors or defects rather than detection or correction or finding a scapegoat.

- Makes available technical literature, relevant data and training facilities.

- Invites visitors to attend the QC meetings or witness the QC presentations.

- Encourages the QC members to make presentations outside the institution.

- Appreciates and recognises QC activities.

- Be prepared for unforeseen risks and introspect if QCs are not functioning well.

- Is beware of over publicity but never keep QCs a "hushed affair".

As highlighted earlier, the most important aspect of the model is "future vision". The management, in addition to monitor the existing QC programme must keep an eye on the future. It is managements' responsibility to look ahead, predict, change the product (Deming, 1997) and expose its staff to the latest developments in the educational arena. It ought to plan what goals it wants to set for itself and the institutions in the coming future.

The Results of The Model

The model when carried out with authentic intent and actions leads to quality education. There is improved employer-employee relationship, improved communication improved work atmosphere, job satisfaction, improved team spirit, enhanced motivation and a sense of oneness with the institution. The use of improved techniques in teaching develops problem solving skills and competence along with increased efficiency and knowledge. Education benefits by giving socially relevant and progressive education and the resultant increased motivation among students, so even problems of poor attendance, campus indiscipline will be automatically solved. Ghanchi (2001) emphasises "the crux of the whole scenario of development is consideration of the human factor as the most important end as well as the means of the process of development".

QC is not a magic wand, though at face value, they may appear so. Applying and practicing QC principles is exacting work. It includes the 'precise definition of roles and responsibilities, appropriate training for all staff to equip them to fulfill their function, the constant review of procedures to guarantee that quality

The Benefits of Having QCs in an Educational Institution

Benefits to the staff/students

(a) Job satisfaction
(b) Provides a sense of participation and ownership
(c) Develops competence and confidence
(d) Builds up team approach to problem solving
(e) Improved work environment

Benefits to the organisation/Management

(a) Development of a complete coherent problem solving methodology
(b) Increased productivity of employees
(c) Enhanced motivation of the employees
(d) Improved quality at work place
(e) Better employer-employee relationship

Benefits for the Society

(a) Gets quality education
(b) Get individuals who are motivated, have ability to solve problems and have logical thinking
(c) Builds national image

problems do not arise and the use of comments from customers to identify and remedy deficiencies as quickly as possible' (Geen et al, 1999). It must be remembered that QC is a part of management's focus on quality. It is neither long term nor short term but represents a permanent feature of focus on quality. As long as the focus on quality is embraced and the right philosophy is adopted, QCs will always show results- tangible and intangible.

A Chinese proverb seems to convey the path of QCs aptly:-

"A journey of a thousand miles begins with a single step."

Making it work- Implementing QCs in Education

A very common question asked about the efficacy of QCs are that 'how can small Circles of 6-10 people solve all the big problems of education?' QCs do not claim to solve "all" education's problems. Instead they significantly improve the quality of education by ensuring better communication, improved working conditions, innovative ways of teaching and learning, better student-teacher relations and making learning and teaching more relevant, practical and usable.

QCs are not just for quality related problems but also undertake problems of personal development. For, e.g., in an educational institution while solving some other problem the QC members felt the need of some personality development course and so they arranged for one!

In a study carried out on 2 Schools, 2 College and 6 University departments of Bombay to assess the feasibility of QCs in educational institutions (Sharma and Kamath, 2003, a), it was found that apart from the management and members, non-members also play a pivotal role in successful QC implementation. Non-members, peers of QC members who were not associated with QC activities played an important part in enforcing the decisions taken by the Quality Circles. Without the support of non-members it is insurmountable to implement the decisions taken by the QCs.

It was observed that 90 per cent of the non-members were ready to help the members to implement any decisions taken during QC meetings as all of them are their friends and they all work together. 70 per cent reported that they have already helped their QC member friends.

These findings are consistent with the findings of Maheshwari (1987) and Srinivasan, (1991) who found in Indian companies, the non-members were indifferent but not resentful of the QC concept and even the union members liked the concept because of its voluntary nature. The attitude of the major trade unions did not show hostility to the QC functioning.

The views of non-members were found to be greatly influenced by their exposure to QC concept. In institutions where the management organized QC introduction programme for a wider audience, non-members had better notions regarding QCs. The institutions where the involvement of non-members was very low or absent reported "QC has had no effect on the members, the members waste their time and ours also, act snobbish, treat us as low and get special treatment". They stated that the members become too critical of everything because of the training received in QC activities. The non-members also commented that the members become 'overconfident, cause disputes among friends and become dogmatic in thinking. They did not think that the QC concept would last long in education.

On the other hand in a college where the QC introduction programme was arranged for the entire staff, there was some basic awareness regarding the QCs concept. The responses to the query "What do you understand by QCs?" were - "It is some problem solving method, brings about some changes, it is a way of getting together and discussing ways to improve self". Non-members of institutions who received exposure to introduction programme but chose not to become QC members reported that the members 'showed' some effect for some period, all of them said that the members look more confident and sure of themselves. They opined that QCs are a step in the right direction for inculcating quality in education but it requires lot of time and support from the management. 43 per cent also stated that the members try to impose more strict rules on staff, it is a way to make life difficult for others, a meeting just for tea and gossip. A non-member commented that she also wanted to join QC but when she sees the 'air of superiority' in others she decides otherwise.

Objections to QC Concept	Potential causes of failure
• Resistance to a new concept • No time • A fear of loss of authority by the management • Members may feel "used" • It is a Japanese concept and does not suit Indian milieu • It will never work. • Skepticism among employees • Members with personal grievances	• Low morale of employees • Lack of training • Selection of QC members and problems by management • Short-term objectives • Incompetent QC leadership • Poor management presentation • Lack of management support • Lack of support of facilities • Management personnel included as Circle members • Circle leaders nominated by the management • Emphasis on faster results

When the non-members who had attended the introduction programme were inquired about the reasons of their not joining the QCs, time constraint was given as a major reason. *Most of such non-members were open to join QCs.* This was in stark contrast to the responses of the non-members who had no exposure to QC functioning and had hearsay knowledge of the concept, who reported that QCs are just a way for the management/ teachers to choose their favourites and make a coterie /prepare students for merit list!

These findings signal that non-members can also be motivated to become QC members. The non-members can be motivated to join QCs when the management deals with them candidly. The results indicate that if the management is determined to make QCs a success, it needs to involve the non-members in the QC programme.

Points of Caution

Prior to the initiation of QCs one must consider certain areas that demand attention. These areas call for special attention so that QCs can flourish.

QC Initiation

- Wherever the focus of QC programme was on individual development, chances of success were enhanced but when QCs were started in haste / with an eye only on the end results the outcomes were disappointing.

- QC activities on a patchwork basis and QC activities which were initiated only to compete with other Circles, were found to give disheartening results.
- Adequate care during each meeting was required so that the members do not develop a feeling of nonchalance.
- QCs were positively influenced when the emphasis was on 'implementation' and not on 'presentation'.
- Sufficient preparation hastened QC success.

Management

- Absolute management support for QCs brought about encouraging results where as lack of support led to absolute disappointments.
- Failure to adequately appreciate improvements by the management deterred the members.
- Sound understanding of QC philosophy on management's part motivated the members to put in their best.

QC Functioning

- The attendance of the meetings by the management members/ principal/outside faculty / visitor resulted in more effective meetings.
- Members' priority to the QC activities depended to a large extent on the interest taken in the QC activities by their immediate department head.

- Lack of understanding of the fundamentals, concepts and purposes of QCs led to loss of interest in QC activities by all.
- Making presentations in front of peers / in conventions boosted the morale and enthusiasm of QC members.

Facilities

- Inability to find time for holding meetings was the primary reason for many not to join QCs.
- Lack of availability of a suitable venue for holding meetings had a deterring effect on the participants.

QC Members

- Synergetic outlook revitalized the QC functioning as against indifferent attitude on the part of some members that prevented others from doing their best.
- Poor attendance in QC meetings was the outstanding cause of QC failure.
- Lack of properly delegated facilitators resulted in unfavourable repercussions on the members.
- Adequate capabilities of the leader herself had a favourable influence on QC activities.

Outside Faculty

- Competent outside faculty was intrinsic to successful QC functioning.

- Management support and importance extended to the outside faculty played an important role in shaping the relation between QC members and faculty.
- QC activities were negatively influenced when they were regarded as the responsibility of the outside faculty.

Non-members

- Non-members' awareness regarding QC activities had a strengthening effect on QC functioning.
- Majority of the non-members were not averse to QC activities.

It is imperative to note that the focus of QC initiation is very important. The focus of a successful programme is 'human resource development', not increasing profits / saving money / or looking good.

Conclusion

Quality is the top agenda of most academicians, and improving quality is probably the most indispensable task facing any institution. Today quality initiatives in education is not a matter of prerogative, it is mandatory. Conscientious and concerted efforts directed at the vast education force in the education system are vital, not only to encourage optimal performance but also to ensure better products capable of independent, analytical thinking and enthused for constructive creativity based achievement.

The quality of education can be enhanced when administration, teachers, staff and education board members develop new attitudes that focus on leadership, teamwork, cooperation, accountability and recognition. Money is not the key to improve the quality of education. The crux of all development is the human factor. The concept of QCs, which is borrowed from the industrial setting, is envisaged to enable key stakeholders to have confidence in the monitoring of the quality of education and management of the outcomes.

Most quality problems are built into the system and the system can be improved only when it is previewed from a Prevention Mindset rather than Inspection mindset. If QCs are to work, they must have the long-term devotion of the senior staff and the institution. QC is not a magic stick, a sprinkling of magic dust. Extending and exercising QC principles is demanding work. As Geen et al, 1999 state it includes the 'precise definition of roles and responsibilities, appropriate training for all staff to equip them to fulfill their function, the constant review of procedures to guarantee that quality problems do not arise and the use of comments from customers to identify and remedy deficiencies as quickly as possible'. It is imperative to recognise this vital fact at all times and under all circumstances.

Two Case Studies of Quality Circles from Educational Institutions: Hands on Experience

A Quality Circle among the Heads of a Higher Education Institute in Bombay

(No. of Meetings Held -28)

(Time for Completion- 8 months)

Average Age for the group – 35 years

Some Select Problems Identified by the QC

- Absenteeism among students
- Absenteeism among peons
- Poor utilization of free time
- Poor college results
- Lack of punctuality
- Noise pollution
- Poor canteen facility
- Crowded staff and classrooms
- Poor communication
- Poor quality of students
- Lack of seriousness for internal examinations
- Poor housekeeping
- Under-utilisation of notice board
- Poor coordination

After mutual consensus it was decided to take up the problem of *"Poor Communication"*

After discussions and brainstorming sessions for around ten meetings the QC enumerated the major causes and sub causes for the problem of "Poor Communication". The major causes identified were-

- Physical environment
- People
- System
- Mode

The cause- effect diagram elucidates the causes and sub causes effectively.

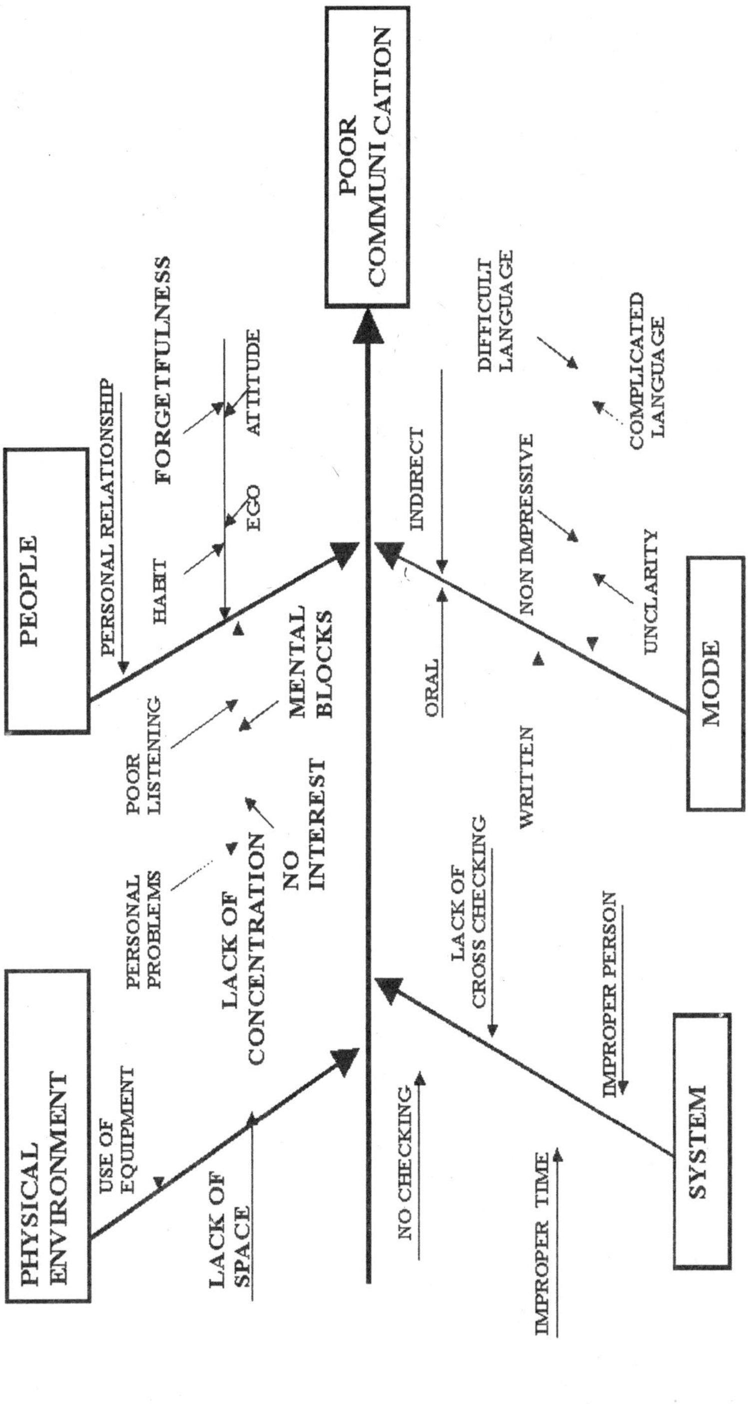
POOR COMMUNICATION
PEOPLE
PERSONAL RELATIONSHIP
FORGETFULNESS
ATTITUDE
HABIT
EGO
MENTAL BLOCKS
POOR LISTENING
PERSONAL PROBLEMS
LACK OF CONCENTRATION
NO INTEREST
PHYSICAL ENVIRONMENT
USE OF EQUIPMENT
LACK OF SPACE
MODE
DIFFICULT LANGUAGE
COMPLICATED LANGUAGE
INDIRECT
NON IMPRESSIVE
UNCLARITY
ORAL
WRITTEN
SYSTEM
LACK OF CROSS CHECKING
IMPROPER PERSON
NO CHECKING
IMPROPER TIME

Action plans for the problems were outlined after brainstorming

Action plan for System

1. Plan ahead and prepare for important communication
2. A personal diary to be kept and all important
3. Inquiry counter with all relevant information
4. After the communication evaluate
5. Right person to be selected for important communication

Action plan for Physical Environment

1. More stand boards / display boards
2. Staff room notice board location to be at more visible place
3. Intercom to be provided at all floors
4. Speakers in all classrooms
5. Telephone operators to be appointed fro better communication
6. Notice board flannel of more attractive colour
7. Schedule for maintenance of equipments to be kept
8. Name boards for heads and laboratories to be provided
9. Every notice to have an expiry date and notices to be removed after that date

Action plan for PEOPLE

To Improve Personality

1. Cultivate positive attitudes
2. Be humble
3. Avoid forgetfulness. Keep notes/ diary
4. While communicating – keep away your ego/ position
5. Appreciate good work
6. Consciously interact with the staff members
7. Actively communicate with the staff

To Improve Concentration

1. Active listening to be practiced
2. Keep personal problems aside while listening
3. Take interest in others
4. Remove mental blocks

Action plan for Mode

For Written Communication

1. Workshop on communication to be arranged
2. Instructions / notices should be brief, simple, precise and eye catching
3. Use of highlighter and coloured chalks for better attention
4. Language should be more friendly
5. Coloured papers to be used for attracting attention

For Oral Communication

1. Practicing listening skills
2. Get feedback on your communication
3. Meeting regularly for once a week for communication on interdepartmental work
4. Respecting each other

The action plan was diligently followed and as a result of QC efforts communication improved in the college. The members reported improved confidence, open-mindedness; they learnt to attack the problem and not the person. They experienced self-empowerment and tried to become positive thinkers. Every head kept a personal diary that was referred to every day.

The institutional benefits were that the learning atmosphere improved, feeling of oneness among staff and heads of faculties improved, work was better organized and a sense of belonging to the institution increased.

More notice boards were put up and notices as well as the notice boards became more attractive. All notices have an expiry date after which the notices are removed. Feed back forms from the teachers for the heads became a routine thing. Intercom facility in the college was provided and an inquiry centre was created. Name boards for the heads of faculties were also made. Workshops for improving communication skills and personality development are organised at regular intervals.

A Quality Circle among the students of class VII of a school in Bombay

(Eight students meeting on Sundays for an hour)

(No. of meetings held -18)

Average Age – 12 years and 6 months

Some Select Problems Identified by the QC

- Lack of concentration in studies
- Lack of active participation in sports
- Lack of discipline at school
- Poor housekeeping at school
- Poor time management
- Heavy school bags
- Sibling rivalry
- Problems in choosing of vocation
- Homework burden
- Peer pressure
- Very high expectation of parents
- Generation gap
- Too many extra classes
- Problems at home

Problems short listed

1. Lack of concentration on studies
2. Bad housekeeping
3. Poor time management
4. Problems in choosing of vocation

Weightage was given to the selected problems and the one with highest one was taken up as the problem for the QC. The problem selected was-

Poor time management

After 5-6 brainstorming sessions on major causes, minor causes and sub causes, the cause and effect diagram was prepared.

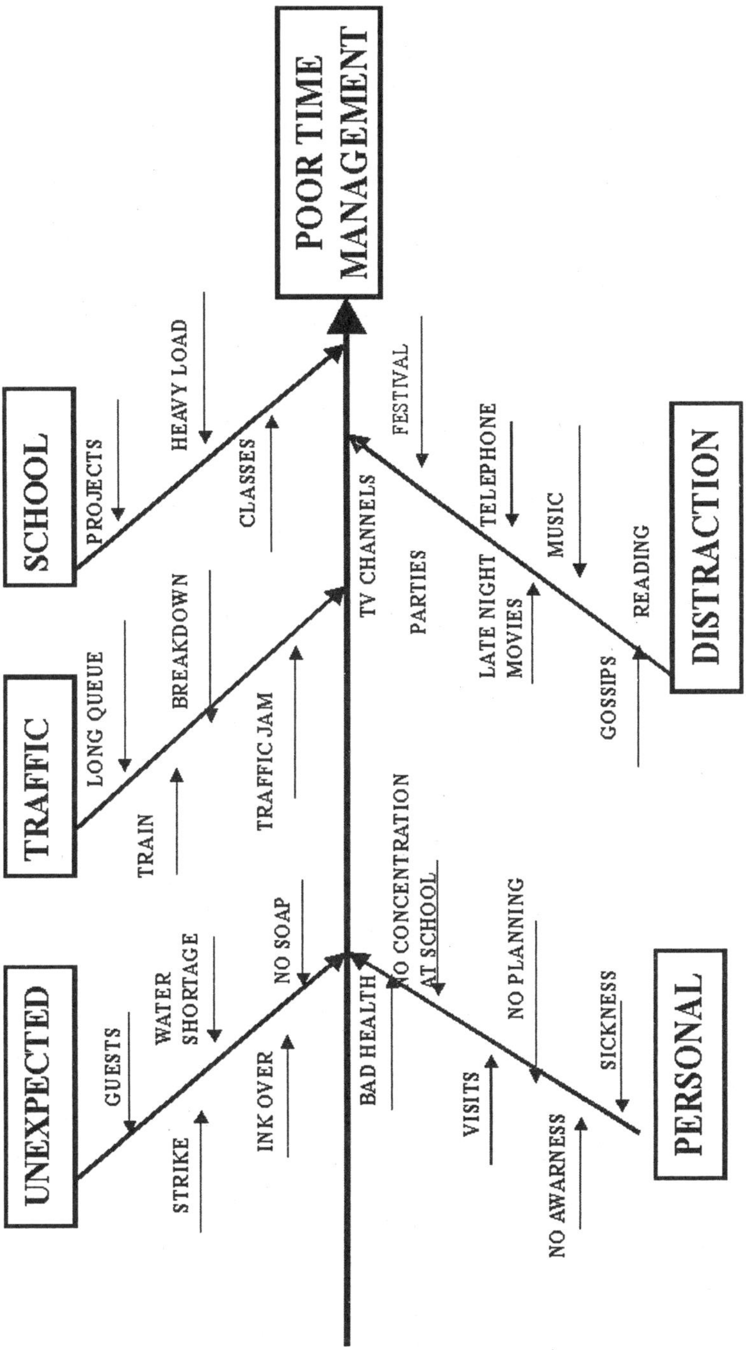
POOR TIME MANAGEMENT
SCHOOL
PROJECTS
HEAVY LOAD
CLASSES
TRAFFIC
LONG QUEUE
BREAKDOWN
TRAIN
TRAFFIC JAM
UNEXPECTED
GUESTS
WATER SHORTAGE
NO SOAP
STRIKE
INK OVER
DISTRACTION
FESTIVAL
TELEPHONE
MUSIC
TV CHANNELS
PARTIES
LATE NIGHT MOVIES
READING
GOSSIPS
PERSONAL
NO CONCENTRATION AT SCHOOL
NO PLANNING
SICKNESS
BAD HEALTH
VISITS
NO AWARNESS

After a lot of deliberations the students prepared a time chart for themselves

Students' Time Table for a Day

Sr. No.	*Activity*	*Until*	*Duration (hours)*
1.	Sleep	6.30 am	8.00
2.	Breakfast and getting ready	7.15 am	0.45
3.	Travel to school	7.30 am	0.15
4.	Attend school	1.00 pm	5.30
5.	Travel back home	1.15 pm	0.15
6.	Change, lunch and rest	2.15 pm	1.00
7.	Home work	3.30 pm	1.15
8.	Extra classes	6.00 pm	2.30
9.	Games	7.30 pm	1.30
10.	Entertainment	9.30 pm	2.00
11.	Dinner	10.00 pm	0.30
12.	Free time	10.30 pm	0.30
			24.00

Flow Chart

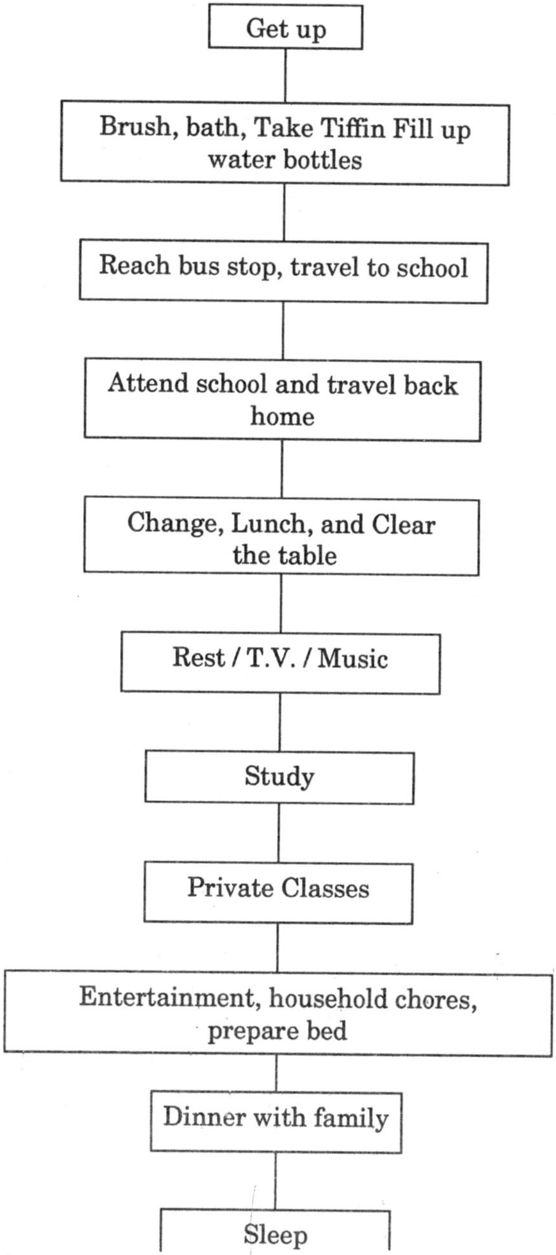
Get up
Brush, bath, Take Tiffin Fill up water bottles
Reach bus stop, travel to school
Attend school and travel back home
Change, Lunch, and Clear the table
Rest / T.V. / Music
Study
Private Classes
Entertainment, household chores, prepare bed
Dinner with family
Sleep

Suggested Remedial Actions for better time management

- Prioritise your objectives
- While taking the breakfast fill the water bag
- While traveling listen to music/ read/ plan for the day or next day
- Talk to your parents while watching T.V./ eating
- Practice science diagrams while watching T.V./ listening to music
- Read fiction while waiting at railway stations or bus stop
- Keep your bags, uniforms and shoes for the next day before going to bed

The students reported having more time at hand, improved attitude, enhanced ability to solve problems, better ranking in the class and improved relations with parents. As they had themselves solved the problems, there was a feeling of ownership.

SECTION- II
GUIDELINES FOR IMPLEMENTATION

Quality Circles (QCs) In Educational Institutions: Select Questions

(For Educationists, Academicians, Administrative Authorities, School / College Managements, Teachers and Learners)

This section of the book emerged as an answer to the needs expressed by the teachers, students and QC experts from industries; stemming from the experiences of and questions raised to the authors during the course of their eight-year research work in different educational institutions in initiating, nurturing, monitoring and spreading QCs.

This section of the book therefore is intentionally maintained in Question-Answer form for ease of comprehension and readability. While a majority of the questions are directly lifted from those asked to the authors, many stemmed from the discussions with persons and situations encountered either at the field or at conferences, meetings, programmes and workshops attended. To underscore certain aspects some parts are reiterated from section–I.

The section is organized to cover questions in the following sections:-

- QCs – Origin, What and Why
- QCs - Structure and Role
- QCs - Managements' Role in QCs
- QC - Non-Members
- QC Activities-How
- QC - Meetings
- QCs - Measuring the Effects of QCs
- QCs - General Issues

QCs- Origin, What and Why

Q. 1.

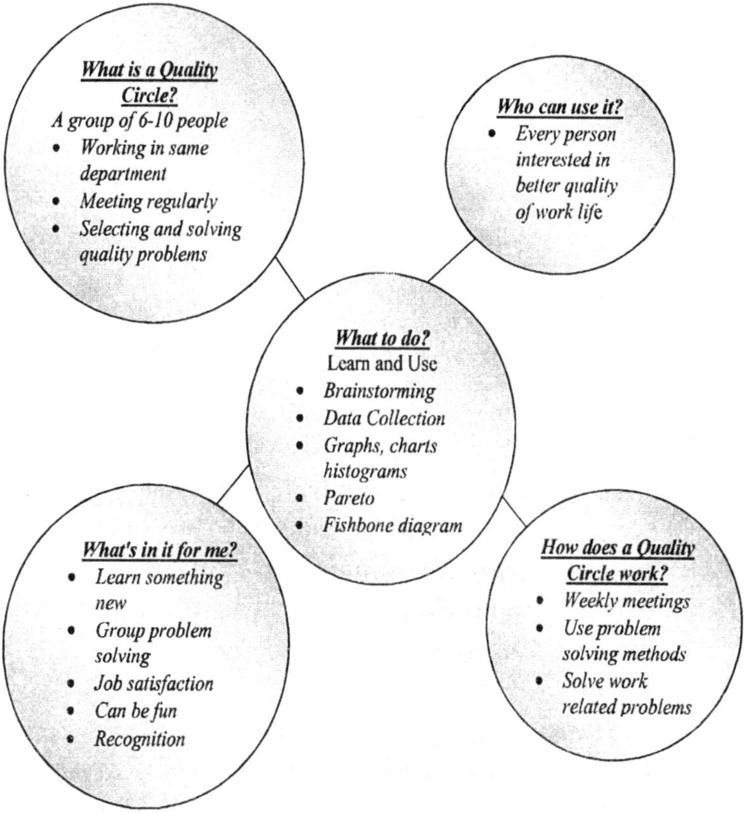

Q. 2. Is it a Latest Fad?

A. 2. Quality can never be a fad. And even if it is, it can be shamelessly embraced! A college principal claimed that because of QCs they have better communication in the college premises, improved space utilisation, a feeling of oneness with the institution and improved team spirit among the staff members.

Q. 3. Why QC in Education?

A. 3. Education is not exempt from the rising expectations of quality. In fact education should be at the forefront-learning, researching, adapting and teaching new knowledge. QCs are a part of an awakening in the education sector towards quality consciousness and quality initiatives. (See Q. 8 for Benefits of QCs)

Q. 4. Have QCs come to Education too late?

A. 4. Better late than never. On the contrary it might be easier and quicker to implement the programme as the pioneering work has already been done, and so ultimately it may even prove to be an advantage!

Q. 5. Is it a Japanese/foreign Technique, to be Redefined to Suit the Education Milieu?

A. 5. Although the concept originated in Japan due to very special circumstances in the years following the war (See Q.13), the philosophy of QC transcends all cultures and has been convincingly proven beneficial almost all over the world. As Dr. Kaoru Ishikawa said, "QC activities which is consistent with human nature – can succeed anywhere in the world as long as its principles are kept and implemented regardless of race, history, social systems or political systems".

Q. 6. We are happy the way we are, why disturb the system by introducing changes?

A. 6. Education has survived the onslaught of external pressure for decades. It refuses to change. But in modern times of globalization, access to foreign education, advanced technology, it is essential to move with the times. By introducing QCs the system is not "disturbed", only "improved".

"We are happy!"

Q. 7. QC is a technique imported from the money oriented business world. Will it suit the "noble profession" of teaching?

A. 7. The QC philosophy (See Q.12) suits every organisation where improvement, progress and zeal for learning is the motto. Even in "money-oriented" business community, the focus of QCs is "individual development" not profit-making. Profits may sometimes result as a by-product of QC activities. In the "noble profession" of teaching QCs are all the more relevant as education is primarily concerned with the "development" of students and making them capable, mature, responsible individuals.

Q. 8. Why should anybody join QC? What is there in it for him/her?

A. 8. Any individual joining QC will be benefited as QCs have the following advantages over other quality improvement methods-

- Everybody participates and contributes in the process of decision-making.
- Problems are chosen, not given.
- Helps in building positive attitudes
- Decision by consensus, not by majority
- Performance oriented, not problem focused
- Promotes prevention- not inspection
- Management blessed, not management directed
- Removes management-worker divides developing common objectives
- Allows a person to become more involved without putting any pressure
- Institution gets a total person

- Harmonious relations at work place
- Brings out extraordinary quality from ordinary people
- Recognizes and taps the intellectual potential of participants
- Development of knowledge and skills
- Promotes creativity among participants. (Also see Q. 73)

Q. 9. Why should the workforce (students/ teachers/administrators) form QCs, after all who is responsible for quality?

A. 9. Quality is a concern of everybody employed in the educational institution, whether they are teaching or non-teaching staff, it is management's responsibility. The staff's contribution can only be guaranteed if the management provides for training, facilities and ambience for quality awareness.

Q. 10. Are QCs meant only for students?

A. 10. No, QCs can work at any level where people are willing to work together and share common

problems. QCs exist among school students; engineering, arts, science and commerce graduates; teachers; lecturers; managements; office administrative staff and even college peons.

Q. 11. How is the QC approach different from traditional management approach?

A. 11. Traditional Management Approach QC Approach

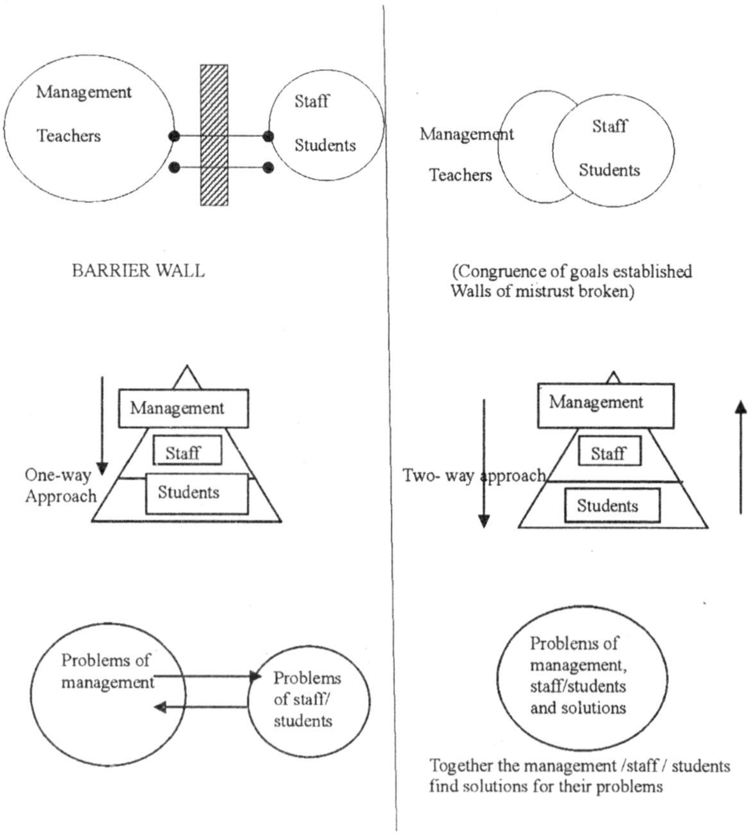

Q. 12. What is QC philosophy?

A. 12. QC activities should continue to progress

- To facilitate every one to fully develop his/her potential
- To create a pleasant work environment
- Where people find true meaning of life.
- To help firms to further develop.
- To promote the material and spiritual level of people
- To contribute to the happiness of all mankind

Q. 13. How and where did the "QC" originate?

A. 13.

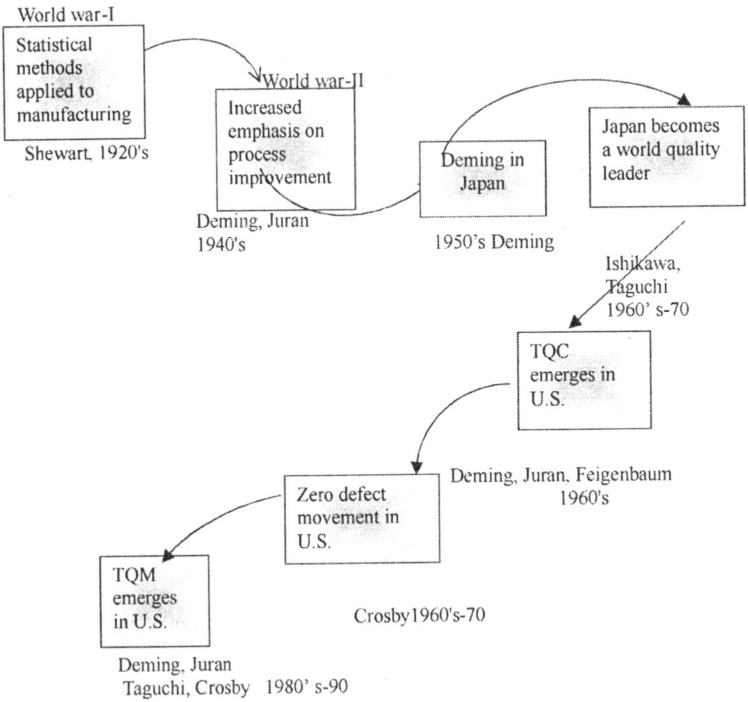

Q. 14. What are the basic ideas/concepts of QC activities?

A. 14. QC concept recognizes

- Respect for humanity and building a happy workplace
- That every person, no matter where in the organisation desires to do quality work
- He/she would like to be respected and would like to contribute to the growth, welfare of the institution
- That the individual on the job has the most knowledge of that particular job
- Teamwork can be more effective and can contribute more than individual effort
- That members must be given opportunity to tap their untapped potentials
- Members' contribution requires recognition
- Training is an integral part to develop the QC movement

Q. 15. What is the code of conduct for members?

A. 15. Attend all QC meetings on time.

- Treat fellow members with respect and affection
- Listen to, and respect, the views of other members.
- Avoid personal criticism.
- Avoid disruptive behaviour.
- Avoid actions that delay progress.

Q. 16. What is the difference between traditional and QC approach to education?

A. 16.

Dimension	QC Approach	Traditional Approach
Teacher's role	Personal, as a friend and guide	Impersonal and distant
Types of objectives to be achieved	Cognitive, emotional and value oriented	Stated and prescribed
Instructional approach	Discovering together and emphasis on learning by doing	One-way, rigid, emphasis on rote learning
Relevance to life	Imparts usable, analytical & practical approach to problem at all fronts	Little
Making a difference	Problem solving in teams, so collective decisions and collective implementation	Each individual is an island. Even if there are good ideas they are not implemented.

Q. 17. What is the role of teachers in the QC programme?

A. 17. Teachers stand at the interface of the transmission of knowledge, skills and values. They shape opinions and develop tastes, helping to form likings and aversions. So teachers play a very important role in the QC

programme. They can themselves demonstrate their commitment to learn, develop and progress by participating in QCs. Also, they can be facilitators for the students' QCs.

Q. 18. How long does it take for the QC concept to show results?

A. 18. QC is a part of management's focus on quality. It is neither long term nor short term but represents a permanent feature of focus on quality. As long as the management embraces quality and adopts the right philosophy, QCs will always show results-tangible and intangible.

Q. 19. What is the status of QCs in the education sector today?

A. 19. QCs have found their way in education all over the world. Countries like Australia, U.S.A., Malaysia, and Singapore have QCs in education. In India, the first QC in education was initiated in 1993 among students from a school in Lucknow. Today there are many QCs in education among students, teachers, lecturers and administrative staff. Many educational institutions in Lucknow, Bombay, Mankapur, Orissa, and Madras have QCs. The latest is an Internet QC formed among students of India and Mauritius.

Q. 20. Even in industries QCs are not always successful. So, what is the guarantee that they will be successful in education?

A. 20. It all depends as to how the institution supports the concept. Any new concept is as successful as the commitment of people behind it. So if the management is really committed failure is a rarity. In industries wherever the QCs have failed the main reason(s) almost always have been lack of commitment from the management or lack of understanding of the concept.

QC is not magic!

(Also see Q. 99 and Q. 100).

Following are the arguments and counterarguments regarding initiating QCs in education.

Why QCs will not work	Why QCs will work
QCs in industries are for improving products but education has no products	Educations' products are even more important than industries'-our students. For the students' and our benefit we must have QCs
QCs will extra ct more work from sincere and simple people	QCs will "empower" sincere and simple people
Education is not yet ready for such concepts	Exactly- so we must make a beginning somewhere!

Why QCs will not work	*Why QCs will work*
There are no targets in QC	That's it. You define your own target and with continuous improvement even keep shifting the target!
It is too much involvement of people	Yes, in education improving human resources is our best bet.
It is too much "talk" and less results.	Only if the concept is not understood properly, this may happen. Otherwise it is the other way round.
It will breed few achievers and dump the rest.	It converts the average into high achievers who have "built in" rewards and motivate the rest to do their best
QCs are an endless agony of teams, meetings, seminars and reports.	It is the highest form of an individual's transformation, a transition both on the personal front and at the work place.

Q. 21. What QCs are not?

A. 21. QCs are not-

- Just for quality related problems but also undertake problems of personal development. For, e.g., in an educational institution while solving some other problem the QC members felt the need of some personality development course and so they arranged for one!
- A forum for grievances or a springboard for more demands
- A means for the management to off-load their problem
- A tool to change the existing organisational hierarchy

- A forum to criticise individuals or department
- A platform to improve others. QCs are for self-improvement, so the problems undertaken are those that the Circle members face and can be solved by changing selves or immediate environment.

QCs- Structure and Role

Q. 22. What is the structure of QC functioning?

A. 22.

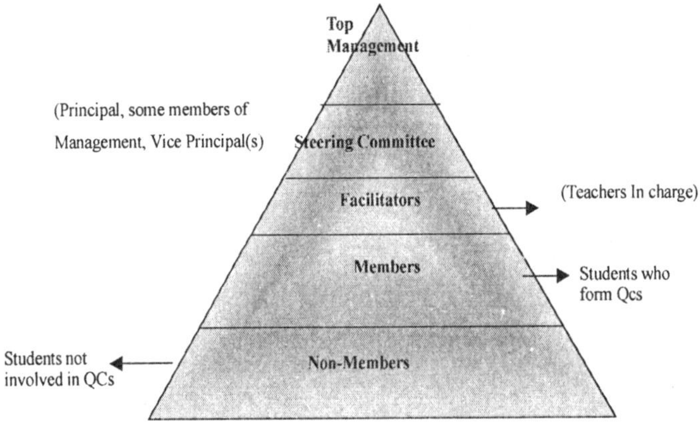

The typical structure of the QCs are as shown in the figure. It depicts the various committees/bodies in an educational institution when QCs are formed only among the students. When teachers/non teaching staff also forms QCs among them then, "members" and "non-members" will change accordingly.

Q. 23. What are the functions/roles of the Steering Committee?

A. 23. Functions of Steering Committee

- Responsible for preparation of objectives for the need of QC in accordance with the institutional philosophy

- Meets regularly with coordinators and guides them
- To identify training needs and promote QC throughout the institution
- To plan launching of QC in every department of the institution
- To provide facilities for QC activities
- To prepare budgets and obtain necessary sanctions for allocation of funds for various QC related activities
- Reviews training and programme materials
- Updates and makes training materials interesting for the members
- Follows up on completed projects
- To give credit to QC teams where due, and organize periodic QC conventions

Q. 24. Who is a Facilitator and what are his Responsibilities?

A. 24. A facilitator is the one who facilitates the process of quality Circle activities. He should have the skill in communicating effectively, perseverance and amiable temperament.

"A facilitator helps you stand on your feet"

The Functions of a Facilitator are –

- To ensure that QCs comply with the guidelines laid down by the Steering Committee

- To participate as an active member of the Steering Committee and act as a link between the Steering Committee and different QCs of the institution
- To train members, leaders, and act as a link between different QCs
- Arrange and attend Circle meetings and maintain Circle records
- Organizes informal gatherings – invites speakers
- To search for new ideas and solve personal problems
- To publicise the concept of QC and motivates non-members to join the movement
- To forward and recommend results/ solutions to the Steering Committee
- To help in preparing for presentations, invitation, papers, visual aids
- To follow up on completed projects

Q. 25. Who is a Leader in a QC and what is his Role?

A. 25. The QC leader is one who directs the QC activities towards conclusion for results. The QC leader is a unanimously chosen member of the QC. His selection is not based on his designation but on his personal traits like leadership qualities, enthusiasm, popularity etc. After completion of one project some other member can become the leader so that every QC member can get a chance to develop leadership skills.

Functions of a QC Leader

- To generate enthusiasm for Circle activities in his/her department
- Delegate work systematically and take care of Circle's operations
- Meet with the Circle once a week
- Use facilitator for assistance and present results/solutions to Steering Committee
- Be responsible for Circle's periodic review reports and progress records
- Creates harmony and coordination in the Circle
- Work closely with seniors and be a key link between management and members
- Enforce code of conduct and keep the meeting on track

Q. 26. What are the functions of QC Members?

A. 26. The QC member is the most vital element in the QC machinery, for without members there are no Circles.

Functions of QC Members

- Attend meetings on time and follow the code of conduct
- Readiness to put in extra hours of work for QC activities
- To learn statistical techniques and contribute to problem-solving
- Promote QC programmes and share information with fellow members

- Motivate new members to join.
- Participate in presentations on QCs

Q. 27. Are Steering Committee Members Volunteers?

A. 27. Partly. The top management as part of the Steering Committee selects members of management who show interest in QC concept. The work is delegated according to their aptitude and capabilities.

Q. 28. To whom does the Facilitator Report?

A. 28. The facilitator normally reports to the Steering Committee.

Q. 29. Should Everything "Go Through" the facilitator?

A. 29. Yes. The facilitator must know of all the developments in the QCs. As he is the link between the workforce (QCs) and management, he should at least be informed of all developments.

Q. 30. Does each QC have its own Leader?

A. 30. Yes. Each QC chooses it own leader by consensus.

Q. 31. Should QCs Always be Formed within a Department?

A. 31. While inter-department QCs exist, many may

not be successful. It is a good idea to have a homogenous group wherever possible.

Q. 32. How are QC Members Selected?

A. 32. QC members are not selected but are volunteers. If more people wish to join a QC than can be accommodated, the alternatives of forming more than one Circle or to reduce the number by some form of lottery should be considered. It is more important to ensure that all QC members and non-members are aware that they all will have the opportunity to become involved in QC activities, if they wish.

Q. 33. What Happens if a Member Wants to Leave the Circle?

A. 33. As the programme is voluntary, people are free to join and leave if they wish to do so. However, such actions are indicators that all is not well and inquiries should be made to understand the real cause.

Q. 34. Are Young Students or Non-teaching Staff Capable of Understanding the Techniques of QC?

A. 34. Of course! The techniques used in QC are simple and easy to understand. There are cases, where Circles, of the age group 8-11 yrs have solved problems with incredible results.

Management's Role in QCs

Q. 35. How Important is Management commitment?

A. 35. As important as water is to fish! Without the top management's genuine commitment, the failure of the QCs is certain and inevitable.

Q. 36. Are QCs a way to Solve Management's Problems?

A. 36. In a way, yes, but in a progressing institution the goals of the management and the work force are the same-improved quality. If everyone is to become involved in the organization, than the problems are of everyone's. With QCs everyone becomes a manager at his or her own level.

Q. 37. What Points should the Management Consider before Introducing QCs in an Educational Institution?

A. 37. The management must do some serious

introspection before starting the QC programme. It should ponder on the following questions and then only take a final decision.

- To what extent it values commitment to the development of the individuals within the system?
- To what extent it values the "we" spirit?
- To what extent it values employees as important members of the organisation?
- To what extent it believes that employees act in the best interest of organisation?

- To what extent it values investing in the development of staff and students?
- To what extent it believes in hierarchy and a feeling that "others" must do their job
- To what extent it values placing decision making as close to the point of implementation as possible?
- To what extent it differs in "espoused theory" and "theory of action/deeds"?

Q. 38. What is the Role of Management in a Successful Programme?

A. 38. 94% of all problems as well as possibilities of improvement lies with the management. Ultimately the management is responsible for the quality in the institution. So, the management has to be really committed and be ready for long-term changes. There can be no short cuts for quality improvements. If QCs are started for decorative or whitewash purposes, they are bound to be a failure. However, a QC programme based on deep understanding and genuine commitment is bound to be a resounding success.

Q. 39. Why should Work-people Trust Management's Motives for Starting QCs?

A. 39. Actually the QCs are meant for staff and students' own development and growth. If people feel being manipulated they can always opt out, as the programme is voluntary! But when people participate and gain tremendous personal benefits, this is not very common. And remember trust is always mutual and infectious!

Q. 40. How can the Management Motivate the Staff and Students?

A. 40. By setting an example itself and living up to the stated policy. If the management is committed, others will fall in line.

Q. 41. Can QCs Create Problems for Management in the form of "Alternative Power Force" in the Institution?

A. 41. No, QCs are not alternate power force or a threat to the management. Instead they are formed to make more effective use of the existing organization. In fact QCs can solve many of managements problems because of improved work conditions, better communication and better management-employee relations.

Q. 42. How do you Maintain Management Commitment?

A. 42. Top management must do it for itself. If QCs are achieving results, this is hardly a problem particularly if the Steering Committee is doing its job and keeping management informed of achievements.

Q. 43. Does Management also Receive Training in QCs?

A. 43. Yes, but only preliminary training. The in-depth training is usually concentrated on the Steering Committee, the facilitator, QC leaders and members in that order.

Q. 44. Do QC Members and Activities Need a "watch" from Management's Side?

A. 44. No! A "watch" from management's side will ensure the death of the QCs and the spirit behind the entire programme. If the members are trained properly, they do not require any control. An atmosphere of trust and faith from management's side will go a long way in making the programme a success.

Q. 45. Can QCs by-pass the Management to Achieve the Results?

A. 45. No, QCs are trained to work within the system, not to create an alternative.

Q. 46. Does a Successful QC Programme Affect the Role of Middle Manager for, e.g., the Heads of Departments and Vice Principals?

A. 46. It will affect their role because they will develop a different relationship with their people, but this is a positive factor.

Q. 47. How do you Prevent Middle Managers from Feeling Inadequate?

A. 47. Some Heads of Department's and middle managers may feel inadequate, especially if they do not appreciate the QC programme but their juniors or counterparts do. The solution is to make them aware of the philosophy, concept, working benefits of QCs. Also, they can be personally counselled for any false notions that they may be harbouring.

Q. 48. Can QCs Work in Institutions where Management-work Force Relations are Poor?

A. 48. Yes, but the failure rate in such institutions is likely to be very high. In such situations, the appointment of a high-caliber facilitator is essential. This, along with the construction of a truly representative Steering Committee with representation from work force and the services of a trained & experienced consultant is essential.

Q. 49. What Happens if the Recommendations cost Money?

A. 49. Although the management has the right to reject a recommendation if it so wishes, rejection is quite rare. This is because Circles are usually very thorough in their work and generally produce extremely persuasive arguments in their presentations. Management may accept recommendations that cost money.

Q. 50. What is the Failure Rate of QCs?

A. 50. The failure rate totally depends upon the quality of the programme initiated. If the QCs are introduced in the right manner the failure rate is low. However even a programme introduced in the best professional way must expect occasional failure of a QC. Failure due to bad implementation is believed to be almost 100 per cent.

QC Non-Members

Q. 51. Who are QC Non-members?

A. 51. Individuals who are unable to join QCs due to any kind of reason(s) are non-members. An effort must be made to slowly involve the non-members in the QC programme for the success of the programme. A non-member who observes QC meetings as a guest may become interested and motivated to join the QC programme.

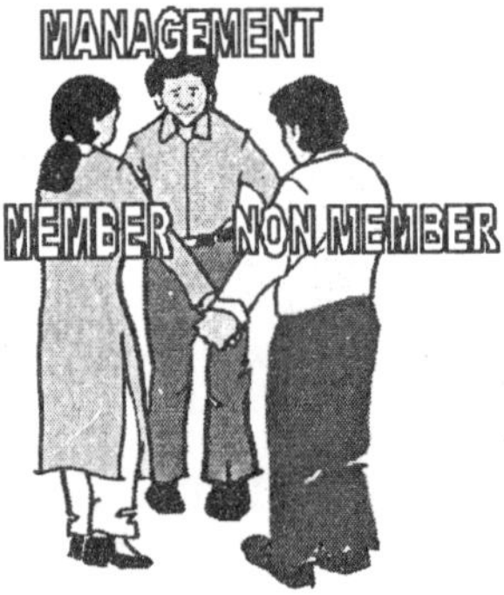

Q. 52. Can there be any Kind of Rivalry-subtle or Otherwise, between QC Members and Non-members?

A. 52. No. If the concept and philosophy of QC is rightly practiced there can be no rivalry. On the contrary a motivated, enthusiastic QC may encourage the non-members to join the Circle.

Q. 53. Will the Non-members Remain so Always?

A. 53. It depends on the QC achievements and the

attitude of QC members in their section. Most non-members are willing to become members if they see an enthusiastic and impressive presentation by their colleagues.

Q. 54. Will Non-members Accept the Recommendation of QCs?

A. 54. Yes, if they are given the opportunity to contribute their own ideas and are kept informed of progress by the Circle. In most cases non-members are very cooperative and many are fence sitters, waiting to join QCs! Also in most cases the recommendations of the QCs are for the benefit of the entire education institution/department including both members and non-members.

Q. 55. What role do Non-members play in QC Functioning?

A. 55. The non-members play a very important role in the functioning of QCs. In the final analysis, the achievement of a QC depends on the extent of successful implementation of ideas generated by the QC members, which depend greatly on the cooperation from non-members.

QC Activities-How

Q. 56. How do you Start QCs?

A. 56. First of all, it is essential to ensure the total commitment of top-level management before starting. Then discussions within the institution with the heads, teachers, administrative staff, unions should be carried out to take them in confidence about your intents and actions. Only then, a facilitator from outside should be called for guidance to implementing the QC programme. QCs can be introduced in an educational institution according to the following steps:

- Appreciation programme for Principals and Teaching staff (Formation of Steering Committee)
- Appreciation programme for Students' Union members (Results in greater awareness)
- Training on tools for students and staff (Formation of facilitators/ coordinators)
- Formation of experimental QC Circle
- Experimental QC Circle's presentation to the Steering Committee

- Propagation of QCs through out the institution

Q. 57. How Long does it Take to Set up a QC Programme?

A. 57. This varies greatly from one institution to another, depending upon circumstances. Normally an institution will be able to form the first QC in about three months from the date of original decision to go ahead, some may take little longer time. Speed is not the important factor. The benefits to be gained from a well-prepared programme will far outweigh any advantage gained by jumping too many fences.

Q. 58. Who Makes Sure that QCs Stay on course?

A. 58. Primarily the QC leader. The facilitator only becomes involved if asked to, by the Circle.

Q. 59. How can Duplication of Efforts be Prevented Among QCs?

A. 59. The facilitator is responsible to monitor such activities.

Q. 60. How does a Circle Select its Problems?

A. 60. Circles choose their own problems and sometimes others can suggest the problems that the Circle may or may not take up.

Q. 61. How is QC Managed by Plan-Do-Check-Action (PDCA) Cycle?

A. 61.

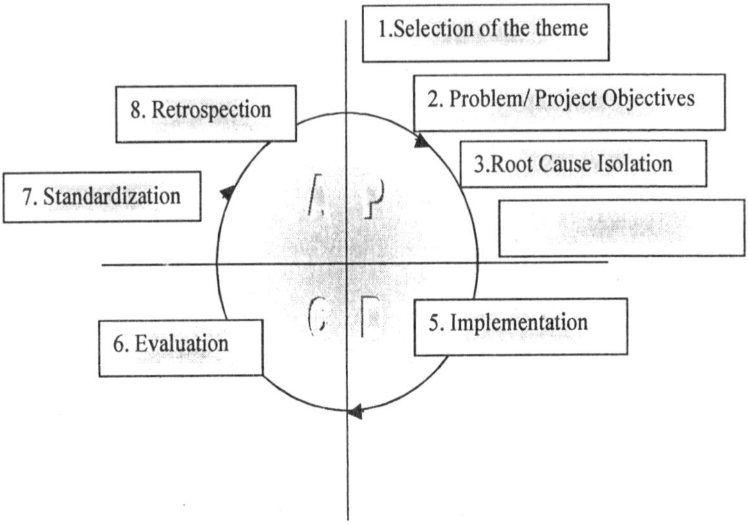

Q. 62. Will QC Activities cause Burden of Extra Work on Employees?

A. 62. The "extra work" that results from QC activities is similar to the resultant "extra work" from activities such as painting, reading etc., the activities one enjoys. QC activities are not a 'burden' as they are voluntary and enjoyable.

Q. 63. What if a QC Cannot Solve a Problem?

A. 63. This is quite rare. Circles can be very resourceful and if it seems that the QC cannot solve a problem, the leader or facilitator may take help from outside. An expert may be called in and his assistance can be taken in solving the problem.

Q. 64. How do Circles Ensure that Problems do not Recur?

A. 64. This is one of the major advantages of QCs over other forms of problem solving. As the problems relate to their own work, the members have complete control of the situation. Problem prevention is one of the most powerful signs of maturity in a developing QC. It is for the members to ensure that the problem is not repeated.

Q. 65. Are there any Considerations before Making a Presentation in front of the Management?

A. 65. Yes, Presentations should be brief. As far as possible all the Circle members should participate. Presentations should be to the point and impressive.

Q. 66. How are Presentations made to the Management?

A. 66. The presentations are usually made to the management after the completion of a project. Sometimes however, an interim presentation may be made, if the project is likely to take long time, or if the Circle needs a management decision before

some aspect of the problem can be studied. Selected presentations may be repeated to other groups such as the Steering Committee, other departments or Circle conventions.

Q. 67. Is Presentation, the End Product of the Project?

A. 67. Solving the problem and successfully implementing the improvement is the end product. Presentation is a way by which management lends its ears to the Circles members and gets acquainted with the Circle activities.

Q. 68. Is it O.K. to Spend a Lot of Time in Preparation of a Presentation?

A. 68. The more impressive the presentation, the better. So spending time for the presentation is essential but care should be taken to emphasize the implementation of the recommendations rather than the presentation.

Q. 69. Who Gets the Recognition?

A. 69. All the members of the group and anyone who may have contributed ideas or assisted the Circle. All Circle members should be encouraged to participate in the presentation, and ideally those others who have helped should be invited to attend.

Q. 70. Is there an Anticlimax after a Successful Presentation?

A. 70. Yes. The more successful the project, the more

the Circle is susceptible to crash afterwards. This is especially true with new Circles. A sense of complacency along with a feeling of overachievement may creep in. However, usually with the support of the facilitator, the Circle can move to its next project and restore momentum.

Q. 71. What are the Problem Solving Tools Commonly used in QC Functioning? Explain.

A. 71. Problem solving can be divided into two stages A. Data Collection, B. Data Analyses

A. Data Collection

1. ***Check Sheet.*** It is a format for documentation/ presentation of relevant data in an appropriate and elegant manner. Data collected thus, scientifically brings out the facts thereby eliminating personal bias. Check sheets may be prepared in the following way

   (a) **Check Diagrams.** Drawings or pictorial views can be employed, preferably among the lower age children Circle members. It marks the location of defects/complaints to find out problem areas.

   (b) **Check List**. A list can be made to make sure that all of the critical items are checked. It can be used in the future. It is necessary that the student members understand the use and need of the good paper work. Check sheet should be simple and useful.

2. ***Histograms And Graphs***. Histogram is a form of column graph, which displays distribution

of values obtained whenever numerical data is collected. Here the values of a continuous distribution are represented by the horizontal axis, which is divided into classes of equal size. Generally, there is one column for each class and the height of that column represents the number of occurrences of data values in the range represented by the class.

Graphs- Graphs are a system of connections or inter-relations among two or more signified by a number of distinctive dots, lines or bars that tells a story without any further explanation. There are many types of graphs used as shown below. It is suggested that these graphs be well explained to QC members for representing the information/data the Circle has collected for its analysis.

(a) *Pie Graphs* are used to show where and what percentage an incident has occurred. The different components of an item are shown in the form of a segment of a Circle. The size of segment represents the percentage, the total being 360 degree. The Pie Graphs are very popular as it is the pictorial representation of data and is enjoyable to make.

(b) *Line Graphs* are the most common of all graphs. They are used to plot things as they happen.

(c) *Bar Graphs* are just like column graphs except that they run horizontally.

(d) *Column Graphs* are just what the name implies and, the vertical column shows the information desired. It is very similar to a histogram.

3. ***Control Charts***. Control Charts provide the user with an indication of stability in the process. It is not recommended for QCs of school level.

4. ***Sampling***. Drawing out of a small group, representative of the larger group of subjects to be studied is sampling. Sampling saves time and cost while giving representative information about the sample to be studied.

   (a) **Random Sampling.** All parts of the data are treated equally and then samples are chosen for evaluation. The procedure of selection could be use of random numbers from tables or odd/ even numbers e.t.c.

   (b) **Stratified Sampling.** It involves dividing the data into two or more groups so that each group can be evaluated separately. Sorting the data thus helps to pinpoint problem areas.

(B) Data Analyses Techniques

1. Brainstorming

It is a technique for generating a large number of solutions in a short space of time, collectively. The underlying principle is that people in groups are able to generate more and better ideas than as individuals. In QCs it is used to identify problems in the first place, analyse causes and for producing ideas for possible

solutions. Also, it is used in a variety of other situations when it is appropriate. It is a powerful technique and when done well can be great fun.

2. *Pareto Diagram*

Pareto Analysis is based on the Pareto principle proposed by Vil Fredo in the 1940's, who had observed that about 80 per cent of the national wealth belonged to about 20 per cent of population. This "80-20" principle or the principle of "vital few and trivial many or useful many" has its ramifications in various fields. In QCs problem solving, this technique is used to make the "vital few" and "trivial many" causes obvious to the observer, to create criteria for the next step, i.e., generating ideas for problem solution and to practice convergent thinking. It is a special bar or column graph. The diagram represents data arranged in descending order from left to right. A cumulative line if used represents the sum of the groups added together.

3. *Cause and Effect Diagram*

It is named after Dr. Ishikawa, professor in the University of Tokyo who first developed it in 1943. It is also called a fish bone diagram because it resembles the skeleton of a fish. It is a very useful technique for the identification of the causes and sub-causes of the problems. It is an organised method of gathering and recording causes of problem. It helps to minimise uncertainties. The Cause and Effect diagram has found immense use among C Circles. It has been observed that most of the problems can be treated as effects of different causative forces which can be categorised under 5"M's- (i) Man, (ii) Machine, (iii) Materials, (iv) Methods and (v) Miscellaneous/ others.

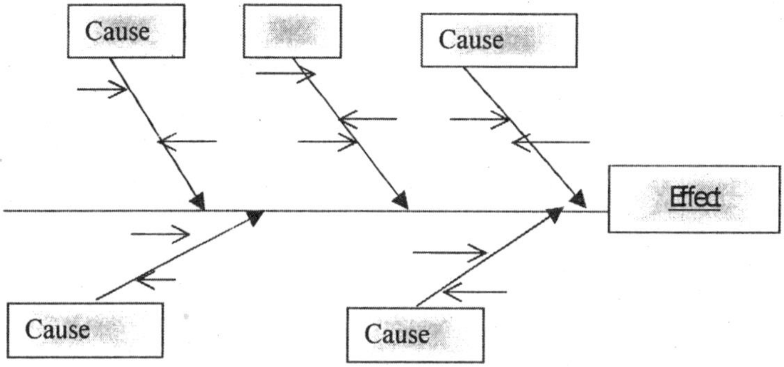

Q. 72. How does a QC Function to Solve a Problem/take up a Project?

A. 72. Following are the steps or stages in solving a problem:-

1. Identify the problem.
2. Collect data/facts about the problem.
3. Analyse the data and find possible alternative solutions.
4. Choose the best solution.
5. Try out the chosen solution.
6. Presentation to the management.
7. Implement the accepted solution.
8. Follow up, monitor and maintain.

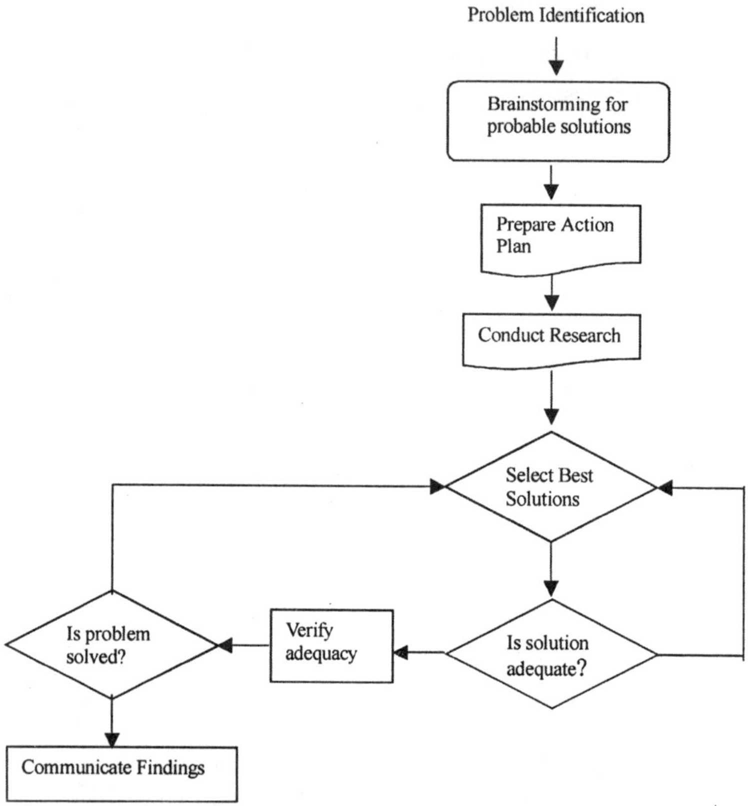
Problem Identification
Brainstorming for probable solutions
Prepare Action Plan
Conduct Research
Select Best Solutions
Is solution adequate?
Verify adequacy
Is problem solved?
Communicate Findings

Measuring the Effects of QCs

Q. 73. What are the Benefits of having QCs in an Educational Institution?

A. 73. **Benefits to the Staff/Students**

(a) Job satisfaction
(b) Provides a sense of participation and ownership
(c) Develops competence and confidence
(d) Builds up team approach to problem solving
(e) Improved work environment

Benefits to the Organisation/Management

(a) Development of a complete coherent problem solving methodology
(b) Increased productivity of employees
(c) Enhanced motivation of the employees
(d) Improved quality at work place
(e) Better employer-employee relationship

Benefits for the Society

(a) Gets quality education
(b) Get individuals who are motivated, have ability to solve problems and have logical thinking
(c) Builds national image

Q. 74. How can the Results of QC Programme be Measured?

A. 74. The results are measured according to the factors considered important by the

management. Usually in an educational institution the factors given importance to are-general attitudes, communication, improved teaching, decreased absenteeism, better work conditions and individual's personal development.

Q. 75. Do QCs Work in Isolation or as an Integral Part of Institutional Activities?

A. 75 Initially, Circle members will tend to work on projects confined to their own work and only involve others to a limited extent. As the QCs begin to mature, they begin to tackle larger projects and involve many others. Ultimately the aim of the QCs is to be in line with the institution's goals and work towards making the institution a quality oriented institution."

Q. 76. What Happens if the Recommendations of a QC are not Accepted?

A. 76. Although every QC member is aware that they can only put up recommendations to the management and the management may or may not accept their recommendations, total rejection of recommendations is a rarity. Normally the management may suggest changes in the proposals. If the management frequently rejects the suggestions or accepts only the superficial ones, members will put their own interpretation for the reasons.

QC-Meetings

Q. 77. Where can the QCs Meet?

A. 77. Ideally there should be separate room for QC activities. But if there are limited resources meetings can be arranged in any room that is free from detractors and noise. Leaders must inform the members about the venue and time at least two days prior to the meeting. No time should ever be wasted for "hunting a room for meeting". This demotivates the QC members.

"Since we cannot find another place, today's meeting will be in the bathroom"

Q. 78. How will the Students/Teachers/non-Teaching Staff Manage the Time for QCs Meetings?

A. 78. Where there is a will, there is a way. In many cases students are known to have waited after school hours, met on holidays/during lunch-breaks, lecturers adjust their lectures and non-teaching staff, adjust their schedules to accommodate QC meetings. The personal gains and sense of achievement will more than compensate for all the trouble taken.

Q. 79. Will QC Meetings lead to even more Unproductive Meetings?

A. 79. No. QC meetings are very different from the general meetings. It is the role of the leader and the facilitator that the meetings are guided towards finding the solution to the problem and there is no wastage of time.

Q. 80. Can QCs Solve Problems of any "Real" Importance?

A. 80. All problems are important if they frustrate the people involved, even though they may sometimes appear trivial to others. In education most of the gains are intangible so the effect of QCs may not be clearly perceived by everyone but the members.

Q. 81. Is One Hour a Week Long Enough?

A. 81. Surprisingly yes. It is amazing how much Circles can actually achieve in a single hour. Very occasionally, a Circle may need longer for some special reasons.

Q. 82. How can QC Meetings be Conducted Effectively?

A. 82. Tips for conducting Effective Meetings

1. **Before the meeting**. Plan- Who should attend? What is going to be the purpose or discussion? Where and when the meeting is

going to be? How long it would be? Prior intimation to members is a must.

2. **During the meeting**. Start and end on time. Reach consensus on agenda. Stick to agenda. Ensure participation of all and encourage it. Assign roles. Encourage listening and thinking. Summarise discussions at least once during the meeting.

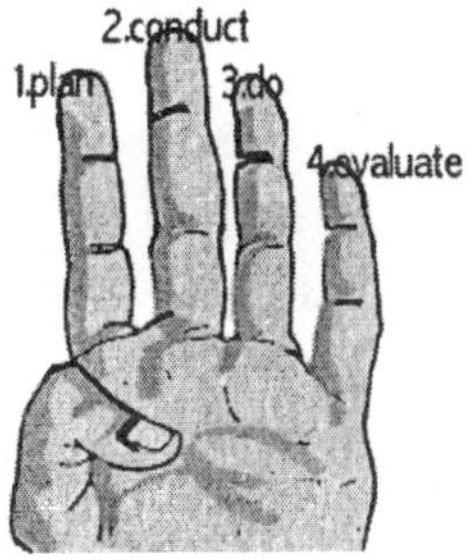

3. **At the end of the meeting**. Summarise and end with a positive note. Draw out action plan. Assign responsibilities to achieve plans/goals.

4. **After the meeting**. Circulate minutes and action plan. Evaluate meeting result to check how purposeful it was.

Q. 83. What are the 'do's' for Teamwork?

A. 83.
- Do leave your grouchy behaviour outside the room
- Do participate in the discussions.
- Do involve teammates, especially the less talkative ones.
- Do rotate the leadership
- Do share the success
- Do weaken the resolve of those who would destroy trust.
- Do commit to making your team effective.
- Do relax

Q. 84. Do QCs Loose Momentum after a while?

A. 84. Yes, they can. It is a facilitator's job to see that they do not. The facilitator should take care to see that the interest of the members does not wane.

Q. 85. What can be done to Keep up the Energy Level of the QCs?

A. 85. Following steps can be taken:-

- Prior to presentation of the present project have a meeting for deciding the next project to be taken.
- Have a win-win attitude. Appreciate others.

- Have an Involvement checklist. Leader or any member of the Circle keeps a list to

General Issues

Q. 86. Are QCs only Concerned with Solving Existing Problems and not a Tool for Innovation and Creative Thinking?

A. 86. This question emanates from lack of understanding of the QC philosophy and concept. QCs solve existing problems in innovative ways. They provide a forum for creative thinking new ideas and innovative styles. In industries, QCs have led to the creation of gadgets, which save time, money & energy.

Q. 87. Will Introducing QCs be a Financial Burden to the Institution?

A. 87. Cost of quality should be measured as the total of what is spent for the overall quality of output. In education the output is not always measurable. Whatever money needs to be spent must be compared with the outcome- increases motivation, increased pride, loyalty and trust, improvements in morale and general attitudes, better work output among others.

Q. 88. Is the Size of the Institution where QCs are to be Started Related to the Viability of the Programme?

A. 88. No QCs can be started in a small school as successfully as in a large university. The mode of operation is identical, and the benefits comparable.

Q. 89. Is it Important to Invite Faculty from Outside the Institution to Train the Members?

A. 89. Yes. Whilst QC appears a deceptively easy concept, it has many technicalities, which cannot be solved with superficial knowledge. An experienced faculty can help by giving expertise and an outsider's objective view to the problems.

Q. 90. What is the Role of the Outside Faculty in Training?

A. 90. A good training faculty will train the members to run their own programme rather than come in and do it for them. Later on he can visit off and on to monitor the programme.

Q. 91. Is there any Point in Starting QC if Good Communication Already Exists?

A. 91. Yes. Such areas are more receptive to

establishing of QCs. They can serve as models for others. Anyway, QCs are not "only" for improving communication. There are lots of other associated benefits.

Q. 92. How do you Convince Everybody about the Programme?

A. 92 You cannot. If there is genuine management commitment at the top and proper understanding of the concept, others will come around to the idea later. Some people will take time to become accustomed to the reality of such a revolutionary change. There may be some who will never accept the concept but they will always be in minority and must be accepted at face value.

"Not by hypnosis!"

Q. 93. How do you get People Interested?

A. 93. Only by presenting the concept in an attractive way and by being honest and dedicated. If the concept is explained well, it is likely to attract sufficient volunteers to get started.

Q. 94. Who Guides or Controls QCs?

A. 94. QCs may be guided but not controlled as such. Within the constraints of the overall programme, QCs should have complete freedom of choice for their activities. The Steering Committee, facilitator, manager or others when requested by the group may give guidance.

Q. 95. Do QCs Require Total Quality Management (TQM)?

A. 95. QCs and TQM are closely related. An organization cannot claim to have TQM unless they have QCs in place. QCs represent approximately 40% of TQM. QCs will more certainly flourish when they are nourished in a TQM environment. There are cases in organisations where QCs are first started without TQM and then gradually a TQM environment is evolved.

Q. 96. How can small Circles of 6-10 People Solve all the Big Problems of Education?

A. 96. QCs do not claim to solve "all" education's problems. Instead they significantly improve the quality of education by ensuring better communication, improved working conditions, innovative ways of teaching and learning, better student-teacher relations and making learning and teaching more relevant, practical and usable.

Q. 97. What Happens when they have Solved all the Problems?

A. 97. To think of a world without problems is inconceivable! Wherever there are human beings, there will be some problems and some solutions. Even if it were possible to have a set up without any such problems QCs will still function because by that time the Circle would have progressed from problem solving to problem prevention and on to improvement and developmentalactivities. There is always something that QCs can do to make improvements.

Q. 98. Are Quality Control Circles (QC)/Quality Circle (QC)/Small Group Activity (SGA)/ Quality Improvement Teams (QIT)/ Quality Control Groups (QCG) same?

A. 98. QC and QC are same, the Japanese insisting on an extra "C" in "QC" to emphasise "control". SGA, QIT, QCG are activities for quality improvement but they differ in some ways from QCs. For e.g. in QIT the teams are cross-departmental whereas in QCs the group is from the same dept.

Q. 99. What are the Obstacles in the way of a Successful QC Programme?

A. 99. **Objections to QC Concept**

- Resistance to a new concept
- No time
- A fear of loss of authority by the management

- Members may feel "used"
- It is a Japanese concept and does not suit Indian milieu.
- It will never work.
- Skepticism among employees

- Workers with personal grievances

Q. 100. What are the Potential Causes of Failure?

A. 100. The most likely causes are:

- Low morale of employees
- Lack of training
- Selection of QC members and problems by management
- Short-term objectives
- Incompetent QC leadership
- Poor management presentation
- Lack of management support
- Lack of support of facilities
- Management personnel included as Circle members
- Circle leaders nominated by the management
- Emphasis on faster results

Q. 101. What can be the Results of Failure?

A. 101. It depends on how and why the programme

failed. Failure can range from the sudden due to the some key support being withdrawn to gentle vanishing in thin air due to lack of interest or support. Either way the results of failure will always be the feelings of "I-told-you-that-this-programme-will-not-succeed" to "Oh-I-am-disappointed-that-it-did-not-succeed". A feeling of loss of motivation may also prevail. So it is very essential that the management explore the need of the programme and its own commitment towards the same prior to induction.

Bibliography

1. Adams, Abha (1996). *Quality in Education, A Paper Presented at CII (Confederation of Indian Industries) Sponsored Quality Summit,* 28th January Delhi.
2. Aggarwal, Rita (1994), *The Magnificent Seven.* The Hitawada, December 28.
3. Amaradasa, Alahendra A. (1999). *Future Trends-Quality Circles Get Renewed Vigour Through the School System.* At International Convention of Students' QCCs at Lucknow in December.
4. American Society for Quality Control in Johnson, R. and Winchell, W. (1990). *Management and Quality.* Milwaukee, WI.
5. Arcaro, Jerome S. (1997). *Quality in Education- An Implementation Handbook.* Vanity Books International, New Delhi.
6. Athshere, Sunil (1996). Paper Presentation at Gujarat State Level Convention on Quality Circles, Vadodara. 7th–8th October.
7. Bagchi, Subroto (1996). Towards World Class. *Management Review,* July-Sept, Oct.-Dec, pp. 16-24.
8. Banks, Jerry (1989). *Principles of Quality Control* John Wiley and Sons Publications, New York.
9. Barlett, B. (1985). Alive But Not Well: Quality Circles. *Production Engineer,* 64, pp. 22-23.

10. Billing, David (1996). Managing Quality Policy and Projects in a University. *Total Quality Management*. Vol. 7, No. 2, pp. 203-212.

11. Bonstingl, John Jay (1993). The Quality Revolution in Education. *Educational Leadership,* November, pp. 4-9.

12. Bradley, Keith and Hill, Stephen (1987). Quality Circles and Managerial Interest. Industrial Relations, *ULCA*, Vol. 26, No. 1 Winter as cited in Mankidy, Jacob (1985) *Quality Circles–Concept, Rationale and Methodology*. Himalaya Publishing House, Delhi.

13. Burgard, Jeffrey J. (1999). *Continuous Improvement in the Classroom.* At International Convention of Students' QCs at Lucknow in December.

14. Chandra, Durgesh and Janakiram, Nanduri (1992). *Quality Circles: Growing Big Through Small Groups.* Tata McGraw Hill Publishing Company, New Delhi.

15. Chandran, S.A. (1986). *Quality Circles – The Technique to Get the Total Person*. Essae Chandran Institute, Bangalore.

16. Chaudhary, Nimit, R. (1996). Higher Education Delivery Systems–Trying the TQM Option-I. *University News*. Sept.16, pp. 1-5.

17. COBSE (1995). *Towards Quality Secondary Education–Agenda for 21st Century.* COBSE in Association with Vikas Publishing House Private Limited Delhi.

18. Cortada, James W. and Woods, John A. (Ed.) (1999). *The Quality Yearbook 1999.* McGrawHill, Toronto.

19. Crocker, Olga L. Chiu, Johnny Sik Leung and Charaey Cyril (1984). *Quality Circles, A Guide to*

Participation and Productivity, Meuthen Press, New York.

20. Crosby, Philip B. (1984). *Quality Without Tears. The Art of Hassle – Free Management.* McGraw Hill, U.S.A.
21. Crosby, Philip, B. (1996). *Quality Is Still Free.* McGrawHill, U.S.A.
22. Dale, Barrie G. (1999). *Managing Quality.* 3rd Edition Cornwell Press, U.S.A.
23. Dale, Barrie G. and Cooper, Cary (1997). *Human Resources and Total Quality–An Executive Handbook.* Beacon Books, New York.
24. Deming, Edwards W. (1986). *Out of Crisis.* Massachusetts Institute of Technology, Center for Advanced Engineering Study, U.S.A.
25. Deming, Edwards W. (1997). *The New Economics for Industry, Government and Education* Massachusetts Institute of Technology, 2nd Edition, 4th printing, U.S.A.
26. Devi, Laxmi Ed (1996). In Chief. *Encyclopaedia of Educational Development and Planning.* Vol. 1. *Education: A Vision.* Institute for Sustainable Development, Lucknow and Anmol Publications Pvt. Ltd., New Delhi.
27. Dewar, Donald (1999). (President QC International). *Team Building Techniques that Work* at International Convention of Students' QCCs at Lucknow in December.
28. Dey, B.R. (1988). *Quality Circles–Concepts and Practices.* McMillan India Ltd., Delhi.
29. Dey, B.R. (1999). Quality Circles: An Indian Approach, Part-II. *Management and Labour Studies.* Vol. 24, No. 1, January, pp. 16-26.

30. Dhantingan, S. (2000). (Sr. Executive, Crompton Greaves) in conversation with the researcher at Confederation of Indian Industries' sponsored QCC Convention, Western Regional Finals. Nashik, Maharashtra, India on 21st January.

31. Diwan, Rashmi (1995). The Quality Revolution–Role of School Leaders in Meeting the Challenge. *New Frontiers in Education*. Vol. 25, pp. 260-273.

32. Dror, Yehuda (1995). The reality of ISO 9000. *Quality Digest*, Sept, pp. 82-87.

33. Duden, Nancy (1995). A Move from Effective to Quality. A Principal Describes Her School's Application of the Deming Approach. *The School Administrator*. June, pp. 18-21.

34. Fabi, B. (1992). Contingency Factors in Quality Circles: A Review of Empirical Evidence. *International Journal of Quality and Reliability Management,* 9(2), pp. 18-33.

35. Feigenbaum, Armand V. (1995). *Leaders in Quality,* p. 173 in Shelton, Ken (Ed.). *In Search of Quality – 4 Unique Perspectives, 43 Different Voices.* Executive Excellence publishing, U.S.A.

36. Fish, Della (Ed.) (1995) *Quality Learning for Student Teachers: University Tutors' Educational Practices.* Fulton, London.

37. Frazier, Andy A. (1997). *A Roadmap for Quality Transformation in Education.* St. Louis Press, Florida.

38. Fu, Guo Gao (1996). *Education and Training–the "Pioneer" for Enhancing the General Quality in the 21st Century Chinese Working People* at International Convention of QCC, Kuala Lumpur, Malaysia. 28th–30th October.

39. Galvin, Robert W. (1995). *Ten Heresies of Quality* in Shelton, Ken (Ed.). *In Search of Quality – 4 Unique Perspectives, 43 Different Voices*. Executive Excellence Publishing, U.S.A.

40. Ganapathy K., Subramanian B. and Nanarayana V. and (1994). *Quality Circles–Concept and Implementation*. QCFI Publication, Secunderabad.

41. Geen, Arthur; Bassett, Phil and Douglas, Lesley (1999). Quality Assurance in School Based Initial Teacher Education. *Education Today*. Vol. 49, No. 2, pp. 94-110.

42. George, P.P. (1993). The Relevance of Today's Education for Youth. *New Frontiers in Education*. Vol. 23, pp. 175-202.

43. Ghanchi, D.A. (2001.) Nation, Destiny and Education. *University News*. Jan. 1, Vol. 39, No.1 pp. 1-5.

44. Ghosh, D.K. (1990). Management Theory in Higher Education System–Application of Norms. *University News*, April, pp. 7-11.

45. Goel, D.R. and Biswal, Ashutosh (1996). TQM in Education: Reality, Desirability and Feasibility. *University News*, Oct. 28, Vol. XXXI, No. 44.

46. Goodfellow, M. (1981). Quality Circle Programmes: What Works and What Doesn't *Quality Progress*. Vol. 14, pp. 32-33.

47. Government of Maharashtra, (1979). *Secondary School Code*. Education, Employment and Youth Services Department. Government Photozinco Press, Pune.

48. Hertzke, Eugene R. and Olson, Warren E. (1993). *TQE, Technology and Teaching*. Corwin Press Inc, California.

49. Holt, Maurice (1993,a). The Educational Consequence of W. Edwards Deming. *Phi Delta Kappan*. January, pp. 382-388.

50. Holt, Maurice (1993,b). Dr. Deming and the Improvement of Schooling; No Instant Pudding. *Journal of Curriculum and Supervision*. Fall, Vol. 9, No. 1 pp. 6-23.

51. Holt, Maurice (1998). "The concept of Quality in Education" in *Quality in Education*. Falmer Press, U.S.A.

52. Horine, Julie E. (1999). *Values for a Quality Culture in Educational Institutes* in Cortada, James W. and Woods, John A. (Ed.). *The Quality Yearbook 1999*. McGrawHill, Toronto.

53. Hutchins, David (1985). *Quality Circles Handbook*. Pitman Publishing Limited, London.

54. ICSQCC (International Convention of Students' Quality Control Circles) held at Lucknow in 18th–20th December 1997 and 15th–18th December 1999.

55. Indriresan, Jayalakshmi (1996), TQM for Effective Educational Management, *University News*, February, pp. 33-35.

56. Ingle, Sud (1985). *Quality Circles' Master Guide – Increasing Productivity with People Power*, Prentice Hall of India Pvt. Ltd., New Delhi.

57. Ishikawa, Kaoru (1984). *Quality Control Circles at Work–Cases from Japan's Manufacturing and Service Sectors*. Asian Productivity Organization, Tokyo.

58. Jayakody, D.J.D. (1996). *TQM as a Process in the Work Environment*. (Additional General Manager, Employees Trust Fund Board, Sri Lanka) at International Convention on QCC at Malaysia, 28th-

30th October.

59. Jayavelu, S. Suganthi, L. Samuel, Anand A. and Jagadeesan, T.R. (1994). *Quality Circles–Its Role and Impact on Indian Industries.* A Research Survey Report by Faculty of Mechanical Engineering. Anna University, Madras.

60. Jaycox, Michael (1996). Team Work: How to Get Non-Believers to Participate in Teams. *Quality Progress.* March, pp. 45-49.

61. Juran as quoted in *Total Quality – Creating Individual and Corporate Success.* (Ed.) Ahluwalia J.S. Institute of Directors, Excel Books (1996).

62. Kaplan, Shankar Sanjay (1990). Introducing Quality Circles in University Administration. *University News,* January. pp. 6-8.

63. Khosla, N.K. (2000). (Sr. Mgr. Bhilai Steel Plant) at Confederation of Indian Industries' sponsored QC Convention, Western Regional Finals. Nashik, Maharashtra, India on 21st January.

64. Konopricki, Patrick (1996). Total Quality-Applied in the Classroom. *The School Administrator,* August, pp. 22-28.

65. Lal, Meera (1994). *Quality Management Through Quality Circles–An Indian Model.* B.R. Publishing Corporation, Delhi.

66. Levit, Steve (1994). *Quality is Just the Beginning,* McGrawHill International Editions.

67. Lewis, Ralph G. and Smith, Douglas H. (1998). *Total Quality in Higher Education.* Vanity Books International, New Delhi.

68. Maheshwari, B.L. (1987). *Quality Circles,* Oxford and IBH Publishing Co. Pvt. Ltd., New Delhi.

69. Marsh, John (1995). The Reinvention of Education.

Quality Digest, Sept., pp. 27-32.

70. Morgan, Colin and Murgatroyd, Stephen (1994). *Total Quality Management in the Public Sector–An International Perspective*. Open University Press, Buckingham.

71. Mukhopadhyay, M. (1997). *Globalisation and Indian Education*, The Pioneer, 9th June.

72. Mukhopadhyay, Marmar (2000). Management of Quality in Higher Education, *University News*. Vol. 38, No. 27, July, pp. 1-5.

73. Mukhopadhyay, Marmar (2001). Total Quality Management in Education, NIEPA, New Delhi.

74. NAAC, (1995). *The Quest for Quality in Higher Education*. Discussion Paper No. 1, National Assessment and Accreditation Council, Bangalore.

75. NAAC, (2000). *Manual for Self-Study for Affiliated Conducted Colleges*, Published by National Assessment and Accreditation Council, Bangalore.

76. Patrick, Manu (1999). Total Quality Management in Fducation. *University News*, Vol. 37, No. 32, August, pp. 1-3.

77. Pirsig, R.M. (1976). *Zen and the Art of Motorcycle Maintenance. An Inquiry into Value*. Corgi. London.

78. QC 117, (2000) QCC presentation at Confederation of Indian Industries' sponsored QCC Convention, Western Regional Finals. Nashik, Maharashtra, India on 21st January.

79. Rafaeli, Anat (1985) as cited in Mankidy, Jacob (1985). *Quality Circles- Concept–Rationale and Methodology*. Himalaya Publishing House, Delhi.

80. Rajput, J.S. and Walia, K. (1997). Quality in Higher Education, *Journal of Higher Education*, Vol. 20 ,

No. 4, winter, pp. 553-567.

81. Rao, C.R. (2000). (Sr. General Manager, Mahindra and Mahindra Ltd.) in conversation with the researcher at Confederation of Indian Industries' sponsored QCC Convention, Western Regional Finals. Nashik, Maharashtra, India on 21st January

82. Rau, R.H.G. (1995). In Inaugural Speech for QCCs Introduction Programme at Smt. P.N. Doshi College of Arts, Ghatkopar, Mumbai on 6th October.

83. Robson, Mike (1982). *Quality Circles – A Practical Guide,* Gower Publishing Company Ltd., England.

84. Robson, Mike (1984). *Quality Circles in Action.* Gower Publications., England.

85. Sallis, Edward (1993). *Total Quality Management.* Kagan Page Educational Management Series.

86. Schargel, Franklin P. (1995). Teaching TQM in an Inner City High School. *Qimpro Quarterly,* January, pp. 14 –17.

87. Shalala, Donna E. (1995). *Quality Education* in Shelton Ken (Ed.) *In Search of Quality – 4 Unique Perspectives, 43 Different Voices.* Executive Excellence Publishing, U.S.A.

88. Sharma, Deepa and Kamath, Ravikala (2002). *Towards Total Quality Education (TQE) Through Quality Control Circles (QCCs) – A Model,* Long Island Education Review, Vol. 2, Issue 2, December, pp. 15-19.

89. Sharma, Deepa and Kamath, Ravikala (2003). *Implementing a Creativity Training Model for In-service School Teachers,* Long Island Education Review , Vol. 3, Issue 2, December, pp. 7-10.

90. Sharples, Kathleen A. Slusher, Michael and Swalm Mike (1996). How TQM can Work in Education?

Quality Progress, May, pp. 75-78.

91. Shelton, Ken Ed. (1995) *In Search of Quality – 4 Unique Perspectives, 43 Different Voices.* Executive Excellence Publishing, U.S.A.

92. Solbai, Samad Bin (1996). *ISO 9000 and TQM as Foundations for Quality Management Excellence.* Paper presented at International Convention on QC Circles at Kuala Lumpur, Malaysia. October 28th-30th.

93. Srinivasan, A.V. (1991). Quality Movement in India: A Status Report, *ASCI Journal of Management.* Vol. 21, pp. 56-75.

94. Stella A. and Gyanam A (2004): *Looking Ahead: A Decade of Accreditation in Retrospect,* AICRA Publishers, Bangalore.

95. Subramaniam, B. (1996). *Quality Circles–Can it be made an Everlasting Movement?* (Director, QCFI) Paper presented at 7th Gujarat State level Convention of Quality Circles, Vadodara 7th–8th October.

96. Subramanian B. Nanarayana V. and Ganapathy K. (1997). *Quality Circles–Concept and Implementation.* QCFI Publication, Secunderabad.

97. Takwale, Ram (1996). IGNOU's Challenges of Quality, Quantity and Equity. *University News,* May, pp. 7-15.

98. Terninko, John (1997). *Step-by-Step QFD Customer Driven Product Design.* 2nd Edition. CRC Press, Florida.

99. Thakur, Manjulla and Nagar, Dinesh (1999). Quality Circles in Public Sector–An Analytical Study. *Indian Management.* October pp. 21-29.

100. Tichy, Noel M. and Sherman, Stratford (1994) *Control Your Destiny or Someone Else Will,* Harper

Business, New York.

101. Tomlin, E. Michael (1994). *In Search of Education's Customer.* The School Administrator, August, No. 7, Vol. 51, p. 16.

102. Tulsi, P.K. (1998). Total Quality Management in Higher Education. *University News,* Vol. 36, No. 25, June, pp. 5-8.

103. Udpa, S.R. (1986). *Quality Circles in India-Participation for Progress.* Tata McGraw-Hill Publication, New Delhi.

104. Udpa, S.R. (1994). *Quality Circles–Progress Through Participation.* McGrawHill, Delhi.

105. Varma, S.K. (1996). *Beyond Excellence Through Quality Training.* Manager-Training at Nippon Denro Ispat Ltd. in Paper Presented at International Convention on QCC at Kuala Lumpur, Malaysia.

106. Venkataiah (Ed.) (1999). *Encyclopedia of Contemporary Education.* Vol. 9, *Management and Quality Education.* Anmol Publications, New Delhi.

107. World Bank Review (1995). *Development in Practice –Priorities and Strategies for Education.* A World Bank Publication, Washington, D.C.

Index

W